THE
POLITICS OF
POVERTY

THIRD EDITION

John C. Donovan

FIRST EDITION Copyright © 1967
by Western Publishing Company, Inc.

SECOND EDITION Copyright © 1973
by The Bobbs-Merrill Company, Inc.

THIRD EDITION Copyright © 1980 by
John C. Donovan

University Press of America, Inc.

4710 Auth Place, S.E., Washington, D.C. 20023

Printed in the United States of America

ISBN: 0-8191-1025-6
Cloth Bound

ISBN: 0-8191-1026-4
Paper Bound

Library of Congress Catalog Card Number: 80-5046

JOHN C. DONOVAN *is the DeAlva Stanwood Alexander Professor of Government and Legal Studies at Bowdoin College, Brunswick, Maine, and was the chairman of the Department of Government and Legal Studies at that institution from 1966 to 1969. He is a trustee of the University of Maine and a member of the board for the Center for Governmental Studies, Washington, D.C. He holds a Ph.D. from Harvard University, and, in 1965, he received the United States Department of Labor Distinguished Service Award.*

As past chairman of the Maine Democratic State Committee, Administrative Assistant to Senator E. S. Muskie, Executive Assistant to Secretary of Labor W. Willard Wirtz, first full-time Manpower Administrator for the United States Department of Labor, and Democratic Congressional candidate in 1960, Professor Donovan's experience in state and national politics has been extensive.

Professor Donovan has written numerous articles dealing with Congress and the legislative process and his book, CONGRESSIONAL CAMPAIGN: MAINE ELECTS A DEMOCRAT, *is a widely acclaimed case study of the successful election campaign of Frank M. Coffin. He has also written, for Pegasus,* THE POLICY MAKERS, *which gives a critical reassessment of American policies of the 1960s and a perceptive look at the 1970s.*

DEDICATED TO
My Family

PREFACE TO THE
THIRD EDITION

THIS CASE STUDY of the Economic Opportunity Act of 1964, representing the initial thrust in President Lyndon B. Johnson's "war against poverty", appeared originally (Chapters One through Eight) in the heat of battle, one might say. The central argument in the original interpretation still stands, now that the dust of battle has settled. LBJ's war against poverty was, indeed, an important victim of the escalation of the other war in Vietnam.

The first edition of the case study was written in 1966, too early to see clearly many of the important aspects of policy-making once this complex set of programs moved into the cumulative processes of implementation. The second edition, which appeared in print in 1974, added Chapters 9 and 10. These chapters reviewed the experience through the Nixon years prior to Watergate. This revised version of "the politics of poverty" revealed the remarkable persistence of most of the original programs, noting their ability to survive years of Presidential neglect, indifference and even outright hostility. In the meantime, the same programs were caught up, of course, in the elaborate, labyrinthine, highly-fragmented, Congressional and bureaucratic subsystems. Year after year, the programs originally laid out in 1964 and 1965 were continuously revised, refined, modified, and in most instances "tamed". Community Action is the best example of a program that soon lost almost all of its potential for effecting important social change at the local level.

The second edition of this case study pointed to the importance of bureaucratic momentum and incrementalism in keeping most of the old Johnson programs alive throughout the Nixon era. (In fact, most of them survived the Ford and Carter years as well.)

If this case study has special merit as a teaching device, it would seem to lie in the fact that it traces a bold Presidential policy innovation through a series of Congressional sessions and follows the programs through the long process of bureaucratic implementation noting the important modifications and transformations which occurred along the way. Finally, it traces the evolution of the same programs through a period when a new President with different objectives decides to blunt his predecessor's domestic initiatives.

Now comes the opportunity, thanks to University Press of America, of presenting THE POLITICS OF POVERTY once again as the nation enters the decade of the 1980's. Young Americans who were yet unborn in 1964 will soon be entering college. THE POLITICS OF POVERTY may serve a useful purpose in helping them gain an understanding of a momentous era of the recent past, some of its brighter aspirations as well as some of its profound failures. Their interest need not be simply antiquarian, however. Although the Office of Economic Opportunity which features so prominently in the case study is long gone, most of its once-innovative programs are still with us: the Job Corps, summer jobs for young people, Head Start, Legal Services for the poor. So, too, are many of the harsh facts. The horrendously high incidence of joblessness among minority youth in the mid-1960's (see Chapter 6 for the grim details) remains virtually unchanged nearly two decades later. But not everything remains the same.

As young Americans of the 1980's probe more deeply, they will also find that the lives of poverty-striken Americans have been affected by other major public policy developments of the recent past: Medicaid providing medical and hospital care for the indigent and Food Stamps for food purchases are prime examples. Medicaid, along with Medicare for Senior citizens, was another Johnson program, while Food Stamps was made available to millions (19.5 million in 1979) for the first time in the Nixon administration.

The politics of poverty is a continuing aspect of American politics and not simply a fleeting episode in the past.

J.C.D.

CONTENTS

INTRODUCTION

LYNDON BAINES JOHNSON, potentially the strongest American president since Franklin Delano Roosevelt, desperately anxious to be another Roosevelt, declared war on poverty in his first State of the Union message. The President warned that it would not be "a short or easy struggle," that "no single weapon or strategy" would suffice. But, he added, "we shall not rest until that war is won."

This declaration by an extraordinarily able political man at the peak of his political powers during one of our rare presidential honeymoon periods inaugurated a new era in the political life of the nation. Coming as it did only a few short weeks after the assassination of his brilliant predecessor, the presidential declaration fell upon the ears of a cooperative Congress which seemed perfectly willing to let the new chief executive have at least one major new program of his own, even though it might be relatively expensive and unorthodox.

Less than three years later, the same president who in the meantime had won the nation's highest office in his own right in a monumental landslide vote and had carried with him an overwhelming majority of his own party into both houses of Congress found his war on poverty in serious legislative, administrative, and political difficulty. Criticism of the operation of the program was intense amidst widespread skepticism concerning the program's purposes. Many of the people whom the program was designed to assist in escaping from the jungle of poverty now viewed it with contempt.

How did this happen? Lyndon Johnson came to the White House after nearly a third of a century in Washington, during which some of the ablest political leaders of our time—Franklin Roosevelt, Sam Rayburn, Harry Truman, John F. Kennedy—had recognized him as a man of rare political skill. How did the one program which bears President Johnson's own distinctive label get into so much difficulty almost before it was off the ground? What caused President Johnson to seize so quickly upon the war on poverty as the central theme of his domestic program? And why did the same Congress which experienced little difficulty in either blocking or emasculating so much of the Kennedy domestic program enact so much of Mr. Johnson's program for social and economic reform (potentially the most significant and comprehensive program since the New Deal)?

Where did the war on poverty originate and in response to what pressures? To what extent was Mr. Johnson's "new" program merely a reworking of proposals well advanced in the days of the Kennedy administration? What were the central concepts of the war on poverty as it was conceived late in 1963 and early in 1964? Who formulated them? Who sponsored them? When and where did President Johnson lose the political initiative and for what reasons? How far did the Johnson administration intend using federal power and federal funds to stimulate fundamental change in the Negro ghettos of the great cities? Does the nation have the resources to fight a two-front war, one in Vietnam, the other in the dark ghettos?

These are some of the basic questions to which this study of the poverty program addresses itself. They all have to do with the politics of poverty. This study assumes that a great new program such as the one brought forth by the Economic Opportunity Act of 1964 does not spring full blown from the head of Zeus—or even the head of LBJ. The war on poverty is helping to reshape American politics. It is the product of an on-going and complex political process, one which begins long before the bill is introduced in the Congress. It involves men in the executive branch, some of whom are not remotely near what is ordinarily thought to be the "policy-making" level. Political and bureaucratic forces begin to shape the bill before it has won White House approval and many of the same forces continue throughout the legislative process on Capitol Hill; there they encounter other forces. The political struggle continues and intensifies after the bill is written into law, especially during the administration of the program. Indeed, the full political potential of the program may not be revealed until the program begins to take effect at the local level—when it hits home.

A presidential declaration of war on poverty is bound to have a profound impact on the status quo. The antipoverty program is certainly going to be unsettling, even if none of its innovations achieves quite the thrust the original planners intended.

What does this portend for presidential leadership? A great deal has been written in recent years about presidential leadership in legislation. We have evolved a twentieth-century presidency in which the initiative is said to have been "institutionalized." As a result, the congressional role in law-making has been substantially weakened—so the theory runs. The Economic Opportunity Act of 1964 is the best example yet of a bill written in the executive branch by the forces represented in the institutionalized presidency.

Is the congressional role in policy-making inherently weak? Is it a minor one? What happens when congressional participation in the making of a law is limited largely to ratifying initiatives taken by the executive? Have we, in fact, reached the point where professionals in the executive branch are able to devise a major new program using essentially esoteric data and make that new program part of the national experience *apart from the workings of the political and legislative processes?* If the technicians come to monopolize the making of a bill, who will defend it in the rough and tumble of political debate? Is it possible—indeed, is it desirable—to effect fundamental reform without conflict and struggle?

These are among the most important questions faced today by serious students of the policy-making process. The findings of this study may suggest that the nature of the struggle between presidential leadership and congressional control is such as to discourage hasty and glib generalizations about the making of public policy.

GREAT SOCIETY EXPECTATIONS

CHAPTER 1

THE BACKGROUND OF A PRESIDENTIAL DECISION: ORIGIN OF THE ANTIPOVERTY PROGRAM

"Wealth to us is not mere material for vainglory but an opportunity for achievement; and poverty we think it no disgrace to acknowledge but a real degradation to make no effort to overcome."

The Funeral Oration of Pericles
THUCYDIDES, *The Peloponnesian War*, VI.

WHEN PRESIDENT LYNDON JOHNSON declared war on poverty in his first State of the Union message, he was announcing the formulation of a new domestic program which he could call his own and which would bear the LBJ brand. The new president, wishing to leave his own mark on history, and having inherited a backlog of unfinished business, wanted an approach and a program which would be uniquely his. Since President Johnson assumed the responsibilities of the presidency at a time when the Kennedy domestic program was stalled on Capitol Hill, there was a natural tendency to view most of the Johnson legislative program as merely ". . . a compendium of programs either started by President Kennedy or at least studied and planned for in his administration."[1]

Where did President Johnson turn for the elements of a new domestic program, one that would be known as the Johnson program?

The historian would probably say that the history of reform politics was the most influential source of the Johnson program. Mr. Johnson is known to be proud of his Populist antecedents; he regards himself as an authentic participant in the great accomplishments of the New Deal. In this connection, we ought not to forget that Franklin Roosevelt made the politics of poverty central to his administration. While Franklin Roosevelt was in part an American conservative who preserved the integrity of the American constitutional system throughout a period of unprecedented strain, and who also conserved the essential edifice of American capitalism, at the same time the political revolution Roosevelt led obviously altered the balance of political forces as the President personally breathed fire and potency into new political groupings.*

Franklin Roosevelt changed the nature of political contests in this country by drawing new groups into active political participation. Compare the political role of labor under the self-imposed handicap of Samuel Gompers' narrow vision with labor's political activism during and since the Roosevelt years. The long-run results were striking: Roosevelt succeeded in activating people who previously had lacked power; national politics achieved a healthier balance of contending interests; and public policy henceforth was written to meet the needs of those who previously had gone unheard. It is extremely doubtful that any of this was lost on Lyndon Johnson, young New Deal congressman from Texas who in later years was fond of saying, "FDR was like a daddy to me."[2]

Lyndon Johnson became an important part of the Democratic congressional machine during the Truman years. President Truman had a natural sympathy for the human welfare aspects of the New Deal and he tried to work within this tradition. Frustrated by congressional opposition, Truman's Fair Deal was not a conspicuous legislative success, although the President used his executive powers with courage and determination in integrating the armed forces. Truman also initiated the struggle over Medicare and managed to keep alive the rhetoric of progressive reform at a time when the country was otherwise preoccupied.

*It is worth recalling that Franklin Roosevelt's first concern was the establishment of economic recovery; his interest in basic reform came later.

The Eisenhower decade of the fifties, a period during which Mr. Johnson emerged as one of the great legislative tacticians in our history, was not quite the total loss some political liberals imagine it to have been. It was, after all, a period in which the substantial gains of the recent past were solidified. Throughout two long presidential terms, the Republican congressional party was never able to launch an all-out offensive against the New Deal. So that issue presumably was lost for all time.

Mr. Eisenhower as president, moreover, took the initiative in the early hours of his first term and encouraged the Republican-controlled Congress to enact the bill which created a new Department of Health, Education, and Welfare. We should be grateful for small blessings. The first Republican president since Herbert Hoover did not abolish the welfare state, but elevated it to Cabinet status!

Nevertheless, it now seems clear that whoever was elected to the presidency in the nineteen-sixties was destined to inherit an unusually large backlog of unfinished domestic business. The only question was how executive leadership might be applied to the growing list of serious national problems. If the nation learned any important political lesson during the nineteen-fifties, it was that strong leadership in Congress (Lyndon Johnson and Speaker Sam Rayburn) was no substitute for strong leadership in the White House. Seen in this context, 1961 to 1963 emerges increasingly as a truly remarkable period. It was, in part, the sheer volume and scope of the many new initiatives which helped to mark this as a creative period in American history. But there was also the revitalization of a tired system as bright, able, energetic, and imaginative people came willingly and with enthusiasm to positions of power and authority in Washington. If the Kennedy men did nothing else, they at least succeeded in thoroughly shaking up the Washington bureaucratic establishment.

In the process, President Kennedy emerged as an eloquent spokesman for a new political generation. In presidential message after message, Kennedy spelled out in more detail than Congress or the country could easily digest the most complete program for domestic reform in a quarter of a century. President Kennedy, however, operated under two severe handicaps. The one of which he was most aware was that he simply did not have the necessary margin of votes in Congress to push through a substantial program of social and economic reform. The New Frontier never had the slightest chance of becoming another New Deal precisely because it lacked the requisite political strength in Congress. Even today, astute students of American politics tend to forget that the election of President Kennedy in 1960 cost the Democrats some twenty seats in the House of Representatives. This basic arithmetic became Kennedy's single largest congressional problem. (The loss of twenty seats means a minus forty voting handicap, since a lost seat counts double.) Arthur M. Schlesinger, Jr. has noted the practical implications:

> He could never escape the political arithmetic. The Democrats had lost twenty seats. . . . All from the North, nearly all Liberal Democrats, nearly all because of the religious issue. Many times in the next two years Kennedy desperately needed these twenty votes. Without them he was more than ever dependent on the South. . . .[3]

The second handicap was, of course, that John F. Kennedy was not to be granted very much time as president—little more than one thousand days as it turned out.

LBJ: MAJORITY LEADER AGAIN

When Lyndon Johnson assumed the responsibilities of the presidency following the assassination, he also faced essentially the same voting handicap in the House, but Johnson knew that for a short time he would have the offsetting advantage of a national mood of cooperation.* History will also record that Mr. Johnson brought to the White House a talent for legislative leadership as great as any in our history, not excluding Jefferson, Wilson, or Franklin Roosevelt. Mr. Johnson wasted not one minute in applying this great talent. Before Christmas, the Congress enacted important changes in the Kennedy-sponsored Manpower Development and Training Act. The new president encouraged enactment of the Vocational Education Act, which promised a revitalization of the whole system of vocational training. Both bills

---

*In the 1962 off-year election, the Democrats regained four Senate seats and lost a net of only two seats in the House—a remarkable feat, surpassing any administration in a mid-term election since 1934. Nevertheless, as Schlesinger points out, the outcome left the internal composition of the Congress little changed. (*Ibid.*, p. 833.)

had been bogged down in a legislative morass for months. Admittedly, these actions were little noted by the general public at the time, but they were small signs of much larger events to come early in the new year. Nor were the December legislative accomplishments lost on all of those Washington influentials and president-watchers whom Professor Neustadt has so helpfully called to our attention.

> The men who share in governing this country are inveterate observers of a President. They have the doing of whatever he wants done. They are the objects of his personal persuasion. They also are the most attentive members of his audience. These doers comprise what in spirit, not geography, might well be termed the "Washington community." . . . In influencing Washingtonians, the most important law at a President's disposal is the "law" of "anticipated reactions," propounded years ago by Carl J. Friedrich. The men who share in governing do what they think they must. A President's effect on them is heightened or diminished by their thoughts about his probable reaction to their doing. They base their expectations on what they can see of him. And they are watching all the time. . . .[4]

The most important legislative problem President Johnson faced was that the great bulk of the Kennedy domestic program was stalled on Capitol Hill with almost no political push left in the system. This included the multibillion-dollar tax reform bill still locked in deadly embrace in Senator Harry Byrd's Finance Committee, a major new civil rights bill, federal aid to education, and, of course, Medicare. Although Mr. Johnson understood the arithmetic of House voting, including the large handicap, he moved ahead as if his congressional margin were overwhelming.

The almost incredible fact is that by the summer of 1964, before he went to the voters in his own right, it was quite clear to the Washington president-watchers that Lyndon B. Johnson was in the process of performing a legislative miracle; that he would be able to get through the Congress virtually all of the Kennedy domestic program, that is to say, the unfinished business of progressive politics going back in fact to the days of Franklin Roosevelt. The Johnson legislative performance in 1964, coming before his impressive landslide victory over Senator Goldwater, ranks with Woodrow Wilson's monumental record as "parliamentary" leader during his first term and in some respects outshines FDR's famous one hundred days in the sense that Johnson had neither the congressional voting strength nor the atmosphere of crisis which so aided Roosevelt in 1933.

Under the circumstances, if Mr. Johnson wanted one program he could call his own—one that would bear the LBJ label—most of the political men in Washington, even Republican congressmen, would most certainly understand and would offer relatively little resistance. Professionals respect superior professional performance.

Two major forces which helped bring into being the Johnson war on poverty are readily identified. Mr. Johnson inherited a backlog of unfinished business in the field of human welfare traceable to Franklin Roosevelt—a tempting prospect for a supremely political man who thought of himself as a protégé of FDR. There was also Mr. Johnson's imperative need, both psychological and political, for a program of his own which was not a residue of the recent glamorous Kennedy era.

If the President's needs were reasonably clear, the pressures on him to accelerate the rate of social change were also extraordinarily strong. The March on Washington late in August 1963 dramatically proclaimed the urgent need in the Negro community for both freedom (the vote) and jobs. Once again the legacy of the Kennedy past was not easily ignored. It was true that the Kennedy-Heller economic policies had managed to lower the overall national average unemployment rate from almost 7 per cent in early 1961 to 5.3 per cent by the end of 1963, but "overall" "average" "national" rates obscure at least as much as they reveal. A 5.3 per cent rate was much too high in itself, but it also tended to hide the explosive reality that unemployment among the non-whites at least doubled that among whites. Unemployment in non-white America was catastrophic, chronic, and malignant, but white America little understood the reality behind the deceptively simple "rate."

What this meant for President Johnson was that when he had succeeded in pushing through the Kennedy civil rights legislation, the Negro might begin to envision that day when he could vote in the South and eat at a lunch counter unmolested by his white neighbors. These are relative gains, to be sure, but they are also simple "rights" which ought to be taken for granted. Thus, the traditional civil rights program which Mr. Johnson inherited seemed remarkably "progressive" in middle-class white America; it was not nearly so impressive in Negro America where one-quarter of the younger generation faced the prospect of a lifetime of unemployment.*

THE JOB CRISIS

In a very real sense, then, the search for the origins of the new Johnson domestic program brings us face to face with the job crisis in which the American Negro found himself in 1963. At the same time that 200,000 friends of the Negro cause converged on Washington in the famous August march and shared Martin Luther King's prophetic "dream," the Kennedy administration was already well advanced in its staff work in building the factual case for a war on poverty. In May, 1963, Walter Heller prepared a memo for the President summarizing and bringing up to date an analysis prepared by Robert Lampman of the University of Wisconsin which showed that the rate at which individuals were moving out of poverty was slowing down. President Kennedy devoted a large part of a June Cabinet meeting to a discussion of the problem of Negro unemployment, and he initiated a series of staff studies on that subject. Throughout the summer of 1963, professionals in the relevant executive agencies—the Council of Economic Advisers, the Bureau of the Budget, the Departments of Labor and HEW—were at work producing what was shortly to become a flood of staff papers. In November President Kennedy advised Walter Heller that he intended to make an attack on poverty a key legislative objective in 1964, in combination with Heller's proposed massive tax reduction.[5]

Ultimately, the result of all of this high-level staff work in the executive branch was to appear in public form in the now famous Chapter Two of the 1964 Economic Report of the President. Chapter Two, as we shall have occasion to see later in this study, presented the data on poverty in America in elaborate and authoritative detail.

If the civil rights crisis provided the immediate political stimulus to President Johnson's war on poverty, and if the staff work was well underway before the assassination, there was also a background of legislative action during the Kennedy years which helped

*A matter thoroughly probed in Chapter 7 of this book.

create an expertise among the technicians and a favorable attitude on Capitol Hill toward public programs dealing with *structural* aspects of unemployment. The decade and a half following World War II produced four economic recessions, each of which was followed in the upswing of the cycle by a higher plateau of chronic, long-term unemployment. When President Kennedy came to the White House in 1961, the fourth of these recessions had left the nation—and the Kennedy administration—with an unemployment rate of virtually seven per cent.*

KENNEDY AND CONGRESSIONAL INVOLVEMENT

The Kennedy administration lost little time in encouraging congressional enactment of the Area Redevelopment Act, which the new president signed on May 1, 1961—the first major legislative achievement of the New Frontier. The new program provided financial and technical aid to those areas with excessive rates of long-term unemployment—so-called "pockets of poverty." The Kennedy administration scored an early (and relatively easy) legislative victory with a bill which was already quite familiar to the Congress. The first ARA proposal had been introduced in the summer of 1955 by Senator Paul Douglas, Democrat of Illinois. On two different occasions thereafter, the bill passed both houses of Congress, but each time encountered an Eisenhower veto. In a real sense, all that was needed for ARA to become law was to find a president who would *not* veto it. Since Kennedy had been a co-sponsor of the bill during his senatorial career, the result was now obvious.[6]

The ARA became law in 1961 largely because it finally won the support of a strong bipartisan congressional coalition which saw the need for a public policy aimed at alleviating long-term unemployment. It was a program conceived and written in the Congress. A year later the Kennedy administration was able to chalk up another legislative achievement as essentially the same bipartisan coalition supported enactment of the Manpower Develop-

---

*There were, broadly speaking, two quite different interpretations of the high rates of unemployment. The "structural transformation" theory stressed the impact of automation and technological change in creating deep-seated and chronic unemployment. This theory led some observers to conclude that "full" employment had begun to occur at higher rates of unemployment than it did in the late nineteen-forties. The "aggregate demand" approach explained high rates of unemployment as the result of a weakness in the expansion of the economy resulting in ineffective demand for goods and services.

ment and Training Act which provided training and retraining for the unemployed. Thus, during the first two Kennedy years, while Dr. Heller and the Council of Economic Advisers were stressing "aggregate demand" theories as a means of stimulating the sluggish American economy, a bipartisan majority in Congress enacted two measures which underscored the structural aspects of long-term unemployment.

It is worth noting also that two congressional subcommittees, one chaired by Senator Joseph Clark and the other by Representative Elmer Holland, both Pennsylvania Democrats, were developing a highly informed and technically sophisticated understanding of the nation's manpower and employment problems. When the time came for a presidential decision to proceed with an attack on poverty (a time of decided triumph for those who had been advocating that economic expansion alone would not eliminate joblessness among the unskilled), there was a vast body of technical data and a considerable understanding of the nature of the problem among key individuals in the executive branch and in the Congress. The technicians were busy preparing new programs to deal with various aspects of the job crisis prior to the assassination of President Kennedy.

Politics, social upheaval, and "professionalized" reform were all moving toward a common point of decision. The evidence overwhelmingly suggests that the nation stood close to a declaration of war on poverty just prior to the assassination of President Kennedy. All that was needed, really, was a decision to incorporate any new program proposals in the State of the Union and Budget messages. Ordinarily that kind of highest level executive decision would be made no later than December. The time had arrived for a presidential decision.

ON THE BRINK OF WAR

Although the press took surprisingly little note of it, actually President Johnson's decision to declare war on poverty was revealed publicly in advance of the State of the Union message. On January 5, 1964, the Office of the White House Press Secretary in Austin, Texas, released a three-page presidential statement on a report the President had just received from the Task Force on Manpower Conservation, a Cabinet-level committee appointed by President

Kennedy on September 30, 1963. The task force was chaired by Secretary of Labor Wirtz; its other members were Secretary Mc-Namara, Secretary Celebrezze, and General Hershey of the Selective Service System.

The President's January 5 statement pinpointed two principal findings of the task force report:

(1) that one-third of the nation's youth would, on examination, be found unqualified for military service; (2) that poverty was the principal reason these young men failed to meet those physical and mental standards.

The President announced: "I shall shortly present to the Congress a program designed to attack the roots of poverty in our cities and rural areas. . . . This war on poverty . . . will not be won overnight."

Coming a few days before the State of the Union message, this was the first public statement from the White House explicitly indicating that the new president had a program of his own which he would present to the nation as a "war on poverty." All of this, of course, soon became abundantly clear in his first State of the Union address where the presentation did have full dramatic effect. The less dramatic January 5 statement concerning the problems of the draft "rejectees" (as they were soon labeled) nevertheless substantiates further the extent to which even Mr. Johnson's "war on poverty" simply reinforced and solidified initiatives which were well underway before the assassination of President Kennedy.

"One-Third of a Nation" was the title given the report of the Task Force on Manpower Conservation, a task force created by President Kennedy late in September. The principal editor of the report—which was to have been submitted to the president before the end of 1963—was Daniel P. Moynihan, assistant secretary of labor, and a Kennedy man. The report was in a very real sense a Kennedy document. It nevertheless was received by President Johnson with enthusiasm, and no one can say that the new president did not make its findings his cause.

CHAPTER 2

THE EXECUTIVE WRITES A BILL

"What are the prevailing ideas about human welfare which are today influencing the policies and the programs of most states in the contemporary world?

"The most important is the changed attitude toward poverty. For many centuries poverty was regarded as inevitable . . . nothing could be done to relieve poverty as a whole. This traditional view was questioned in Britain during the closing years of the 19th century and challenged with growing insistence in the 20th. . . . An important aspect of the new attitude was that poverty became for the first time a subject of scientific investigation and intellectual inquiry. The methods of the social sciences and new statistical techniques were called upon to aid political leaders and social reformers who were seeking to solve the age-long problem by means of governmental action."

WILLIAM A. ROBSON,
The Governors and the Governed (1964).

ONCE THE President made the decision to declare war on poverty and to bring forth a new legislative proposal which would encompass a set of programs bearing a distinctly LBJ brand, the actual preparation of the bill became a major, all-consuming effort on the part of high-level executive staff people, most of whom were several layers removed from the President.

The Council of Economic Advisers, as we saw earlier, had been at work for some time preparing a staff analysis which was to provide a profile of poverty in the United States. The Bureau of the Budget, which has the central responsibility for preparing the president's budget and his legislative program, had already received from the executive departments scores of specific suggestions either for new programs or for means of implementing existing activities. In addition, there were certain legislative proposals which had been introduced in Congress as part of the Kennedy program still on the Hill awaiting action. The Youth Employment Act, for example, introduced in the Eighty-eighth Congress as S1, proposed a two-pronged attack on the problems of jobless youth between the ages of sixteen and twenty-one. Title I of the act would establish a youth conservation corps, and Title II would authorize the secretary of labor to assist states and cities, by means of grants, to develop local community service occupations. There was also the possibility of establishing a national service corps—often referred to as a "domestic" peace corps—although this had been so much a special Kennedy family project that a new president might find it difficult to impose his imprint.

There is reason to think that the White House at first inclined in the direction of using these legislative items from the Kennedy past as vehicles for the new Johnson program. The January 5 presidential statement endorsing the "One-Third of a Nation" report, for example, specifically called for the enactment of the Youth Employment Act. There were also words of praise for the national service corps concept. In fact, the President went on to say: "I will include funds for them in the forthcoming budget."

Thus, as late as January 5, 1964, the presumption would have been that President Johnson was about to place the weight of his office and his own legislative skill behind two more Kennedy measures, the Youth Employment Act and the domestic peace corps, which were bogged down on the Hill, just as he was to do for civil rights legislation, the tax cut, aid to education, and Medicare. The need for a brand new omnibus antipoverty bill was neither obvious nor certain in the first days of January, when it was not yet clear that the President wished to have a major new program which he could call his own.

It now seems reasonably clear that President Johnson decided shortly after January 5 that he wanted a new legislative proposal to support the declaration of the war on poverty which was announced in his State of the Union message on January 8, and that the new approach was to provide for a broader attack on the causes of poverty than would have been possible under the Youth Employment Act and domestic peace corps proposals.

SHRIVER'S TASK FORCE

On January 31 President Johnson announced that he had asked Sargent Shriver, director of the Peace Corps, to serve as his special assistant in developing strategy for the war on poverty. Shriver brought to his new assignment the aura of Peace Corps success, a quality of creative imagination, a talent for public relations and salesmanship, and a solid reputation on Capitol Hill. He was a dramatic personality, a man with a reputation as a practical idealist who "gets things done." Shriver in turn immediately obtained the services of Adam Yarmolinsky from the Defense Department, Daniel P. ("Pat") Moynihan from the Labor Department, and James Sundquist from Agriculture to serve as his task force in preparing the new bill.

The choices are interesting. Yarmolinsky was special assistant to Secretary Robert McNamara; a brilliant young lawyer, Yarmolinsky was considered an authentic "whiz kid." He had worked before for Shriver, in the period prior to the Kennedy inauguration, as a key member of the talent search team. During the six months in which the poverty program moved through the legislative labyrinth, Yarmolinsky was to become Shriver's principal deputy, in fact if not in name. Pat Moynihan, a liberal New York intellectual-politician, had first worked as an Averell Harriman staff man in Albany, later served as assistant to Secretary of Labor Arthur Goldberg, and was appointed assistant secretary of labor upon the recommendation of Willard Wirtz shortly after Mr. Wirtz succeeded Goldberg in the Cabinet chair. Sundquist came to the Shriver task force from the Office of the Undersecretary of Agriculture, where he served as the principal deputy. This might be slightly misleading inasmuch as Sundquist was also a former Governor Harriman aide who had served in the White House during the Truman years and who had also served most recently as administrative assistant to Senator Joseph Clark, the Senate's leading spokesman on manpower and employment issues.

When President Johnson decided to initiate a major new domestic program of his own, it was a team of Eastern liberal intellectual-politicians under the leadership of a member of the Kennedy family establishment which was given responsibility for formulating it. No one from Texas played a key staff role in the formulation of the antipoverty legislation with the possible exception of Bill Moyers, who was presumed to be close to Mr. Shriver as well as to Lyndon Johnson.

There is by this time a legend in the making which grossly over-simplifies reality. The legend suggests that Yarmolinsky, Moynihan, and Sundquist, presumably with Sargent Shriver looking over their shoulders, wrote the Economic Opportunity Act all by themselves. There were other important participants in the process, one may be sure. Among them: Wilbur Cohen, the peripatetic assistant secretary for legislation in the Department of Health, Education, and Welfare. Cohen was not only one of the nation's leading academic experts on social security legislation, he was also a skilled lobbyist with a reputation for looking after HEW's bureaucratic empire; he was not likely to sit quietly in a corner when a significant new education and welfare program was in the making. The professional staff of the President's Committee on Juvenile Delinquency was a key group. It was true that it tended to be composed of men who had been selected by Attorney-General Robert Kennedy, and that the juvenile delinquency committee was considered a Robert Kennedy special activity; on the other hand, the committee's professional staff collectively represented most of the expertise in the federal government in what was to become "community action," a significant concept in the new program. Inevitably, there also were important, though often publicly anonymous, men from the Bureau of the Budget, that all-powerful, elite presidential staff agency which was not likely to let an *ad hoc* Shriver-led team take over completely a Bureau of the Budget function, the development of new legislation for the President. After all, the Bureau of the Budget had a new boss, and it was anxious to show Mr. Johnson what *it* could do.

There were other agencies and departments which had bureaucratic interests to protect as well as ideas to offer. Chief among them were Labor and HEW, whose views presumably were represented by Moynihan and Cohen, respectively. The others: the Council of Economic Advisers, Interior, Commerce, Agriculture, Justice, the Small Business Administration, and the Housing and Home Finance Agency.

But Mr. Shriver alone had the presidential mandate, and he was in charge. No one ever doubted that important fact. Since Mr. Shriver was known to have no great receptivity toward old-line bureaucrats, even old-line agencies soon learned to keep that type away from him. To an exceptional degree, then, the forces Shriver represented in this operation were those of the presidential-Cabinet policy-making group, which at this time was still overwhelmingly Kennedy in style, inclination, tempo, and mood.

In typical "Kennedy" fashion, the men of the Shriver task force lost no time in turning to idea men outside government for specific program concepts, especially as they soon discovered that the ideas emanating from the executive departments reflected a great deal of conventional wisdom and more than a little bureaucratic self-interest.

The most influential program concepts came from economist Robert Lampman, foundation executive Paul Ylvisaker, Mitchell Sviridoff, a community leader from New Haven, Connecticut, and the technical experts on the staff of the President's Committee on Juvenile Delinquency. It was Lampman's studies of the incidence of poverty which Walter Heller used to document his original brief in May and which also led the way to the chapter on poverty which appeared in the President's 1964 Economic Report. Ylvisaker, who was in charge of the public affairs program for the Ford Foundation, pioneered the development of the "gray areas" program which in turn helped pave the way for the community action program in the Johnson war on poverty.[1] It was Ford Foundation money which underwrote the successful series of pilot projects in New Haven, and it was in New Haven that a talented group of people, led by Mayor Richard Lee and Mitchell Sviridoff, put together what is perhaps the best local community action program in the nation. In addition, there was the small staff working for the President's Committee on Juvenile Delinquency, which had developed relationships with nearly every significant program of social experimentation in the leading cities. This was the intellectual and professional "bank" whose resources Sargent Shriver was to draw upon most heavily in drafting the Economic Opportunity Act of 1964.[2]

During the search for ideas which could be translated into program concepts, Shriver and his small team of assistants also heard, as one might expect, from church, labor, business, farm, and academic and civil rights spokesmen.* In view of what was to become a difficult issue later, it is worth noting now that the American poor

*At the time the bill went to Capitol Hill, the administration released a list of 137 names, described as "a partial list of people Mr. Shriver consulted in developing the poverty program."

themselves did *not* participate in the process which led to the creation of the act. (It goes almost without saying, of course, that it is in no way rare that the poor did not participate in the design of a major administrative proposal for legislation.)

The men who wrote the draft bill in the executive branch worked against awesome time pressures. Shriver was given the assignment on January 31; the bill went to the Hill on March 16. The discussion and negotiation process in bill-drafting is inherently time-consuming. The Shriver style of work encouraged sessions which typically ran into the late evening hours. The remarkable fact is that in about six weeks the task force, aided by a group of legal draftsmen from various executive departments headed by Assistant Attorney-General Norbert Schlei, were able to put together a bill which was ready to go to the Hill. Ordinarily a routine updating of an established department's legislation might be expected to take six months in the drafting.

The Economic Opportunity Act of 1964 represented an interesting mixture of old and new. Although the bill in its original form carried six titles, only two are of major importance to an analysis of the political potential of the war on poverty. Title I established three youth programs, two of which differed only slightly from similar provisions in the Kennedy youth employment opportunities bill which had been passed by the Senate and reported by the House committee before languishing in the House Rules Committee. The third youth program, a work-study program for college students, had been considered earlier as a possible amendment to the National Defense Education Act. Title II, on the other hand, bearing the label "Urban and Rural Community Action Programs," was without precedent as a legislative matter. Under ordinary circumstances, a new multimillion-dollar proposal coming to Capitol Hill for the first time would be certain to receive careful scrutiny by appropriate congressional committees, regardless of program content.

The origin of the community action concept in the executive branch is an important part of the analysis in the next chapter, but it is worth noting now that the idea came from the staff of the President's Committee on Juvenile Delinquency.[3]

If it is difficult to understand the influence of professionals in the formulation of a key legislative concept with such an obvious political potential, it may be that Mr. Shriver found this particular group easy and natural to work with because of the close ties to Robert Kennedy's office. But it is additionally significant that key people in the Bureau of the Budget, after looking over all of the program suggestions from the various executive departments, were disappointed to find little that was strikingly new—until they hit upon community action which was being actively propagated by the juvenile delinquency committee staff. At least part of the responsibility for community action and "maximum feasible participation of the poor" should be assigned to the Bureau of the Budget, without whose support these new ideas might not have found their way into the Economic Opportunity Act, certainly not in the form of a $315 million allocation during the first year. This may help explain the firm parental interest which the Bureau of the Budget later displayed in community action, even in public, an unusual posture for this non-publicity-seeking presidential staff agency. Bibby and Davidson, in their study, go further; they suggest that Bureau of the Budget and juvenile delinquency staff people encouraged Robert Kennedy to get in touch with a somewhat skeptical Shriver. According to this version the Attorney-General ". . . persuaded [Shriver] to emphasize the Community Action programs as Title II of the new bill."[4]

CONGRESS RATIFIES LBJ'S PROGRAM

The first opportunity for congressional influence to be felt in the development of the Johnson administration's antipoverty program came in the House of Representatives where the Ad Hoc Subcommittee on the Poverty Program, a subcommittee of the House Education and Labor Committee, opened hearings on March 17 under the chairmanship of Congressman Adam Clayton Powell. The committee made relatively few changes in the bill. In part this can be accounted for by the way in which Republican committee members were turned aside. Republicans on the House committee, led by Representative Peter Frelinghuysen of New Jersey and Representative Charles Goodell of New York, who had often been able to offer suggestions for amendments to similar proposals in the past and occasionally win committee acceptance, now learned that Mr. Shriver was not interested in Republican-sponsored amendments to the administration bill. Mr. Shriver was more than ever the President's spokesman inasmuch as the President had announced the day the bill went to Congress that Shriver was to be his chief-of-staff in directing the war on poverty.

Since nothing had occurred to alter the basic arithmetic of voting on domestic issues in the House (except the advent of Mr. Johnson to the presidency), the blunt turning aside of Representative Goodell and his group seemed unusually provocative. Further intensifying anxieties was the announcement that Congressman Phil Landrum of Georgia was to be the chief sponsor of the bill in the House. Landrum seemed hardly the ideal choice from the viewpoint of civil rights leaders. Organized labor remembered that Landrum had played a key role in the Landrum-Griffin Labor Reform Bill in 1959, a bill generally thought to be antilabor.

Although there were muffled groans from a few professional liberals, Andrew Biemiller, chief lobbyist for the AFL-CIO, made no public protest. The tactical plan seemed clear. Northern administration loyalists would obviously vote for a bill so close to the President's heart. Landrum was to help line up a sufficient number of Southern votes to make this a Democratic program. If ambitious young Republicans wanted to oppose a war on poverty in a presidential election year, so be it. This was the strategic pattern within which the Economic Opportunity Act was sent to the Congress. It is hard to imagine that such a daring strategy was set by anyone other than the President himself.

The House Ad Hoc Subcommittee heard testimony from a long parade of witnesses, most of whom favored the bill. From the President's official family came Shriver, Heller, McNamara, Celebrezze, Wirtz, Hodges, Freeman, Kennedy, Weaver, Foley, and Udall. Their testimony was largely in terms of generalities; the questioning, by and large, was anything but probing. If this was the program the President wanted, the Democratic majority on the committee was not interested in creating any special obstacles in the spring of 1964.

Seventy-nine witnesses appeared during twenty days of House committee hearings, seventy of them speaking in favor of the bill. The Chamber of Commerce, the National Association of Manufacturers, and the American Farm Bureau Federation predictably found little merit in another welfare "spending" proposal. In view of later developments, there is some irony in the fact that five mayors, including Mayor Richard Daley of Chicago, urged prompt passage of the Economic Opportunity Act.

Although it would be almost impossible to imagine a legislative proposal with a greater potential for arousing congressional anxiety than community action, Title II came through the Congress intact in 1964. Attorney-General Robert Kennedy, administration spokesman for Title II, testified before the House committee. He had this to say about the "maximum feasible participation" requirement:

> The institutions which affect the poor—education, welfare, recreation, business, labor—are huge, complex structures, operating far outside their control. They plan programs for the poor, not with them. Part of the sense of helplessness and futility comes from the feeling of powerlessness to affect the operation of these organizations.
>
> The community action programs must basically change these organizations by building into the program real representation for the poor. This bill calls for maximum feasible participation of residents. This means the involvement of the poor in planning and implementing programs: giving them a real voice in their institutions.[5]

Community action provided a direct financial relationship between the federal government and the local community. The federal funds might even go to non-governmental groups, including those at the neighborhood level. Community action encouraged the development of local projects whose purposes might well include the stimulation of fundamental change in urban ghettos and in slum schools. Title II explicitly proposed that this was to be carried on with "maximum feasible participation" of poor people in local neighborhoods. (Congressmen might have been expected to read this "in local *precincts*.") In community action the revolutionary aspects of the war on poverty came to a focus; power was to be given to those not included in any establishment.

Oddly enough, Congress did not probe the potentially explosive Title II. Congress in 1964 either did not understand community action or it did not bother to take a close look.[6]

This is not to suggest that the Congress did nothing. It was Congress which added two new programs—aid for adult literacy education and assistance for migrant farm workers. Representative Edith Green (Democrat of Oregon) insisted that the Job Corps be open to women as well as to men. The House committee came dangerously close to reviving the church-state controversy when a compromise was reached under which parochial schools could receive aid for non-sectarian "remedial non-curricular" programs. The House committee Democrats had no difficulty voting down a Republican alternative bill sponsored by Representative Frelinghuysen. The House committee also eliminated a program of incentive loans to businessmen.

The portion of the bill which drew the greatest congressional resistance had to do with alleviating *rural* poverty, and the greatest pressure to amend that portion (Title III) was felt not in the House where the voting was thought to be close, but in the Senate where the administration's strength was great. The Senate leadership agreed to delete a provision authorizing outright grants to impoverished farmers, and substituted a loan program. The Senate also accepted an amendment sponsored by Senator Frank Lausche (Democrat of Ohio) which deleted a plan to set up farm development corporations to buy blocks of land to be sold at lower prices for family farms.

SHRIVER AND THE SOUTHERN CRITICS

The Senate passed the Economic Opportunity Act (S.2642) in a 61-34 roll call vote on July 23. The House passed the bill in amended form on August 8 by a roll call vote of 226-185, a wider victory margin than the White House expected. Representative Landrum, powerfully aided by White House muscle, converted a good many Southern members to the cause of social reform and community action as 60 Southern Democrats joined 22 Republicans and 144 Northern Democrats to form the House majority. Only 40 Southern representatives voted "nay." They were joined by 145 Republicans.

The administration paid a price for some of this Southern support. There was, first, the matter of a gubernatorial veto which originally appeared as a Senate amendment and was later incorporated by Representative Landrum in the House version. In its final form, the veto applied to Titles I and II, giving the governor thirty days to review any proposed projects within his state.

Sargent Shriver paid an even higher price for Southern support. Adam Yarmolinsky who was slated to become the deputy director of the new Office of Economic Opportunity somehow had attracted the active animosity of several Democratic congressmen.

The so-called case against Yarmolinsky will probably never be known, but it is a fair guess that it resulted from a mixture of labels—"leftist," "abrasive," "intellectual," and "whiz kid" among them. The terms of the deal upon which the Southern congressional critics insisted were simple; the price of their support in the House was that Yarmolinsky was to have no part in the administration of the new program.[7]

As time went on, there was reason to believe that Shriver may have paid a higher price than, perhaps, he had originally realized. Yarmolinsky was almost the only man in the embryonic Office of Economic Opportunity who knew where all the pieces in the jig saw puzzle were located. Time and again, Yarmolinsky alone had represented Shriver in complex high-level negotiations with federal departments and with the Bureau of the Budget; only he knew the precise terms of a number of detailed administrative arrangements which went to the heart of the operations of an enormously complicated new program. Indeed, Yarmolinsky sometimes appeared to responsible operating officials in other agencies to be the only Shriver subordinate who could speak for his boss with any real authority and make it stick. In any event, from that day forward, Mr. Shriver evidently has had great difficulty finding a deputy with whom he could work. As we shall see when we come to the actual administration of the war on poverty, Mr. Shriver appears to be the kind of inspirational leader who needs a strong deputy.

The congressional role in developing the Economic Opportunity Act was essentially a minor one. The evidence supports the judgment that ". . . Congress was asked not to draft the war on poverty, but rather, to ratify a fully prepared Administration program, and invited, though hardly encouraged, to propose marginal changes."[8] The Economic Opportunity Act moved from drawing board to enactment in just about six months. It is doubtful that any single piece of domestic legislation of similar importance and scope had moved so rapidly and easily through the Congress in a quarter of a century. One would have to go back to FDR's one hundred days in 1933, that classic time of executive dominance over Congress, to find a clear precedent.

The Economic Opportunity Act is a prime example of executive legislation; it was written in the executive branch and subsequently endorsed by the Congress. It is part of a twentieth-century development in which the president's role as "chief legislator" has been "institutionalized" not only in the sense of establishing the congressional agenda, but also for proposing the specific content of bills. One result is that "the classic legislative function—bringing political combatants together to hear their claims, and then resolving these claims—is becoming, in the complex modern polity, less and less the exclusive domain of Congress."[9]

What does this portend for the vitality of the legislative branch? We have tended to believe that political bargains are struck in the Congress; the executive, according to this view, ratifies the bargains when the president signs them into law and when the bureaucrats begin to administer the programs. Is the tendency now to reverse the traditional institutional roles? If the pattern we have seen at work in the origins of the Johnson war on poverty were to prevail, what would the congressional role become?

Perhaps it would be wise not to bury Congress prematurely. The congressional role in writing the antipoverty program was indeed a minor one in 1964, but the circumstances were highly unusual. Congress did add two programs and emasculate another; it did provide for a gubernatorial veto—of sorts. Likewise, Congress, through the work of its appropriations committees, cut back the funds for the first year from $962.5 million to $800 million. Furthermore, Title I of the Economic Opportunity Act borrowed heavily from a Kennedy youth bill which had passed the Senate and moved as far as the Rules Committee in the House before Mr. Johnson assumed the presidency.

Only Title II was strikingly new, and it *was* the creature of the executive branch. Its unprecedented use of federal funds and federal encouragement to arouse the poor against established political organization and established welfare and educational bureaucracies scarcely received a glance from the Congress in 1964.

The important question raised by the example of the Economic Opportunity Act is: what is the congressional attitude in the long run likely to be toward a program it did not help create, once that program stirs "controversy"?

CHAPTER 3

COMMUNITY ACTION: POOR PEOPLE AGAINST CITY HALL

"The first and strategic step in an attack on poverty is to see that
it is no longer self-perpetuating."
JOHN KENNETH GALBRAITH.
The Affluent Society (1958).

WITH THE EXCEPTION of the youth programs in Title I, which
borrow heavily from the Kennedy administration version of
the Youth Employment Opportunities Act, it must be said that
community action, as it appears in Title II of the Economic Opportunity Act provides not only the largest single program in the
Johnson antipoverty attack but also represents an innovation of
surpassing importance. Title II also has a direct impact upon urban
politics in this country and at its most sensitive points.

Perhaps it is not completely remarkable that community action
moved so effortlessly through the first congressional round without
stimulating either congressional curiosity or anxiety. Title II, when
read casually, sounds pedestrian enough:

Section 202 (a)

The term "community action program" means a program—
(1) which mobilizes and utilizes resources, public or private,
of any urban or rural, or combined urban and rural geographi-
cal area (referred to in this part as a "community"), including

but not limited to a State, metropolitan area, county, city, town, multi-city unit, or multi-county unit in an attack on poverty;

(2) which provides services, assistance, and other activities of sufficient scope and size to give promise of progress toward elimination of poverty or a cause or causes of poverty through developing employment opportunities, improving human performance, motivation, and productivity, or bettering the conditions under which people live, learn and work;

(3) which is developed, conducted, and administered with the maximum feasible participation of residents of the areas and members of the groups served;

(4) which is conducted, administered, or coordinated by a public or private nonprofit agency (other than a political party), or a combination thereof. . . .

One develops a certain amount of sympathy for the men in Congress when he realizes that he has just read language which is loaded with political dynamite; Section 202 (a) (3) is the famous section which stipulates "maximum feasible participation" of the poor (although it does not read "the poor") and thereby stimulates a process of major social change. It all sounds innocuous enough when phrased by the legal draftsman.

Actually, there were only a few people in Washington early in 1964 who had any very clear notion what community action in fact was. Most of them were professional staff employed by the President's Committee on Juvenile Delinquency, a group which had been assembled by, and had been working directly for, David Hackett, a close personal friend of, and special assistant to, Robert Kennedy. Once again, the war on poverty which President Johnson so much wanted to make his own was in actuality both the creature and the captive of the Kennedy past in its most vital aspects.

This is not to suggest that community action as a concept was totally unknown outside Washington. It had a few academic sponsors, principally Richard Cloward and Lloyd Ohlin of Columbia University's School of Social Work, whose work on juvenile delinquency challenged the social welfare establishment. Lloyd Ohlin was especially close to the staff of the President's Committee on Juvenile Delinquency. David Hackett, the committee's executive director, has been quoted as saying that Ohlin ". . . was the single most important influence on me."[1] Paul Ylvisaker of the Ford Foundation had pioneered in the development of an operational form of community action. There was a working example in New Haven, thanks in part to Ford Foundation support. Governor Sanford, using Ford funds, was experimenting with community action across the entire state of North Carolina. There were interesting pilot projects in most of the larger cities. But, by and large, *federal* expertise was limited to members of the JD (as it was called) committee staff.

To other federal officials working on the initial phases of the war on poverty, community action occasionally seemed the incantation of a mystical cult. By reading, and even more by listening, one learned a few salient features: community action was fervently anti-establishment; schools, employment services, welfare agencies, city hall were all part of an "establishment" or "system" which served "the disadvantaged" (another key concept) by referring them from one "helping service" to another without ever really understanding or challenging "the culture of poverty" and with no real ability to move families and individuals out of poverty. Community action involved the use of federal funds to exert pressure on local bureaucracies, to encourage them to innovate and challenge them to create new institutions. Community action was a means whereby the poor themselves would participate in formulating and administering their own local programs of social reform.

MAXIMUM FEASIBLE PARTICIPATION OF THE POOR

While it is quite clear that Congress played no part in developing the stipulation that the poor themselves should participate to the "maximum feasible" degree, the precise manner in which the concept found its way into the draft legislation is not nearly so clear. People who were active in the drafting stage acknowledge that "participation of the poor" came directly from the staff of the President's Committee on Juvenile Delinquency. At least one person who was part of the Shriver task force was unable to recall any extended discussion concerning "participation of the poor." The tendency now is toward the belief that the task force thought principally of the *Southern* Negro simply because they had difficulty imagining how community action might reach poor Southern Negroes unless the

Negroes were themselves active participants in shaping the local program. I have been able to uncover no evidence, even "circumstantial," which indicates that the Shriver task force inquired deeply into the probable implications which "participation of the poor" in community action in *Northern* urban ghettos might have. Whether the issue was ever sharply posed for presidential decision will perhaps never be known. One does wonder a little, though, whether President Johnson, as a political man, would have had much enthusiasm for Section 202 (a) (3) if it had been suggested that such a specific legislative mandate to involve poor people would bring his administration into sharp conflict with, let us say, Mayor Daley of Chicago the moment it became operative.*

Whatever its political impact may be, community action is potentially an important instrument of social change, and yet, oddly enough, few Americans have any awareness of its meaning, much less its relevance. Community action is perhaps best appreciated if it is contrasted with prevailing community welfare efforts. The setting is almost any Negro ghetto in any big city. The description is taken from Glazer and Moynihan's little classic, *Beyond the Melting Pot:* "Perhaps the worst misfortune of this bottom layer in New York," they write, and they might have added, in Rochester, Philadelphia, Atlanta, Los Angeles, Chicago, or Cleveland,

is the need to deal with large numbers of harried city employees who have no contact with each other, or, in truth, with their clients, except for the specific malfunction which brought them into action. The school teacher or principal can do nothing about what goes on at home; the welfare investigator's role must be simply one of testing whether the family is qualified; the probation officer is supposed to keep in touch with his case, not the case's family, and can do nothing if the home in which the probationer is located is in a tenement that is a center for drug addiction or thievery; the housing project employee (if the family is lucky enough to be in one) is concerned with financial eligibility, the payment of rent, and the maintenance of the physical property; the hospital hands out drugs and treatment; and so on and so on. And social workers and others now and then set up a joint project to see if out of the welter of bureaucratic confusion there can be fashioned an

---

*A question we come back to in the final chapter of this book.

instrument that responds to families and individuals as full human beings.[2]

Community action is a technique for mobilizing the resources of the whole community to respond to families and individuals as "full human beings"; it tries to find a way through the "welter of bureaucratic confusion." Viewed in this way, community action appears to be essentially a means of effecting a greatly improved "administration" of overlapping welfare and training programs in the local community.

If only it were so easy to keep "administration" and politics hermetically sealed off from one another!

The truth is that the men who pioneered the development of the community action technique as staff members of the President's Committee on Juvenile Delinquency during the Kennedy years went beyond mere "administration" in their objectives. It was their belief that a program which would effectively attack deeply rooted economic and social inequalities must necessarily involve the development of groups among the poor capable of exerting substantial political pressure on existing institutions.[3]

From the very beginning, many members of the professional staff in Mr. Shriver's office who had responsibility for administering Title II of the Economic Opportunity Act operated on the assumption that the involvement of the poor in policy-making was necessary in order to redistribute power in the cities; without power redistribution, they believed, there would be no great improvement in the lot of the Negro poor. In the words of an OEO workbook, "One of the major problems of the poor is that they are not in a position to influence the policies, procedures, and objectives of the organizations responsible for their welfare." White middle-class Americans long ago learned all that there is to know about organizations, policies, procedures, and objectives. Poor Negroes find the words themselves devoid of meaning. From the start of the new program, one of the central objectives of Mr. Shriver's staff has been to correct this condition of *powerlessness,* to place the poor in active roles in their own projects, including the making of policy.

JITTERY MAYORS

The first to recognize this simple fact were the denizens of city hall, who have been understandably jittery ever since. On the other hand, the militant leaders of the urban ghettoized poor are hardly delighted at the prospect of merely attending more committee meetings. Even though the antipoverty councils in large metropolitan cities such as New York, Chicago, and Philadelphia, for example, increase the number of council seats available to poor people, skeptics point out that the poor are nearly always outnumbered by the articulate and politically skillful representatives of powerful organizational interests. What is needed, argue leaders of the New Left, is a sharpened concept of involvement, namely, that the poor and their "real" leaders must acquire *the power to control the funds* and the policies of the local antipoverty programs. It is time to do away with "welfare colonialism" in America, they maintain.

Richard Cloward, one of the influential academic voices who helped develop community action as a going concept, has minimized "mere" policy-making as a means of involvement:

> Membership on policy-making bodies may confer a little prestige on the poor persons who participate, but it will do little more than that when they are outnumbered by the representatives of powerful organizational interests. Indeed, having been granted representation on citywide antipoverty councils, they now seem vaguely uneasy about their victory. They begin to sense that they have been victorious on the wrong battlefield, or at least on a relatively nonstrategic one.[4]

Increasingly, "community action" and "maximum feasible participation" become focal points in a vast, continuing political struggle between big-city mayors and militant leaders of the urban Negro poor. The stakes could hardly be higher. We tend to forget that mayors are a considerable force in American national politics with its tradition of decentralization within the party organization. After all, Richard Daley is not only the mayor of Chicago, there is no more powerful Democratic politician in the entire state of Illinois.

Mayors resist "maximum feasible participation" for reasons which are not exactly ideological. If new representatives arise among the non-white urban poor, they will surely undermine the power of the men now entrenched in city hall, whose power, especially since the nineteen-thirties, has depended in no small measure on control of the "welfare industry" and the millions of federal dollars that flow through city hall en route to the poor. Yet, mayors are resourceful men; they have to be. Only a highly untypical mayor would turn his back on the kind of money which is available under Title II, coming as it does on a 90-10 matching basis. Most mayors enthusiastically seek these new federal funds which OEO has to offer; if at the same time they manage to meet OEO standards without overly encouraging the development of new groups in the ghettos which will threaten their own hegemony, so much the better, from their point of view. Very few politicians, high or low, prefer to oversee the liquidation of their own empires.

Stated crudely, mayors as a group would like to maximize the flow of federal antipoverty dollars into their cities while minimizing the degree of federal intervention in local customs. If the mayor is big enough and strong enough, he may add a number of new projects which increase the number of city employees significantly, thus strengthening the mayor's political organization.

Obviously, few mayors today are in a position to use federal antipoverty funds simply as a means of oiling their machines. The typical American mayor sits on top of an active volcano. The new militant Negro spokesmen in the urban ghetto are precisely the people who are seeking ways of increasing pressure on city bureaucracies for better schools, housing, and jobs. Consequently, the mayor—even Mayor Daley—is far from being a free agent; no matter how great his power or how strong his political machine, he needs the new federal programs in order to keep the volcano from erupting.

There is no reason to assume that mayors as a group are "evil" men or even that they are inordinately insensitive to the needs of the poor. Unfortunately, the typical mayor finds himself placed between the militants in the ghetto and those whites who have only recently made *their* way out of the city slums, and who feel threatened by the forces below them on the social ladder. Many mayors face a serious political problem when the white working class on whom they depend for support turn sullen or violent against what they regard as Negro inroads. Even "liberal" mayors (Richard Daley is in many respects an impressive mayor) who have been charter members of the New Deal and the New Frontier find it politically difficult to go all the way with the Great Society as it tries to relate to the Negro revolution.

NEW HAVEN'S MAYOR LEE

The tragedy is that so few mayors are able to view the new anti-poverty program in anything other than a "hold-the-lid-on" perspective. Yet, at least one mayor has shown that it is possible to rebuild the community and at the same time strengthen his own political position. Mayor Richard Lee of New Haven has managed to keep at least one step ahead of the social revolution rather than wait for the riots to overwhelm him. The New Haven experience is instructive, and, in some respects, it may be unique.

New Haven is not a large city in the sense that New York, Los Angeles, and Chicago are, and although New Haven has its share of poor and underprivileged people—including disadvantaged Negroes—its problems lack the massive weight of the big-city dark ghetto. Thanks to Mayor Lee's leadership and foresight, New Haven had a head start on all the rest. New Haven has had available, first from the Ford Foundation and then from the federal government, funds on a scale which has made it possible to move beyond a series of unconnected pilot projects. Mayor Lee hired and encouraged some of the best professional talent in the United States—Mitchell Sviridoff, Edward Logue, Howard Hallman, Thomas Appleby, and George Bennett, all of whom, incidentally, have since moved from New Haven to large cities. Lee carefully wooed and won the New Haven power structure.* It was no disadvantage either to have the rich resources of Yale University near at hand, and Lee came to the mayor's office from the administration of the university. Most important of all, Dick Lee has viewed the rebuilding of New Haven as a political undertaking into which he has poured in generous volume his own zest and capacity for political action.

The experts have tended to view New Haven as the model for community action, and one can easily see why. It has one drawback as a model, however. New Haven was not a pioneer in placing poor people in policy-making roles. New Haven makes effective use of poor people in its programs; its programs reach people who desperately need help; it employs people from the poor neighborhoods as non-professional community workers. In these respects the model merits emulation. Policy-making is another matter, and

---

*I am aware that Robert Dahl's study of New Haven, *Who Governs?* (New Haven, 1961), found a series of overlapping elites rather than a single power structure. Whatever it is, Lee tends to carry it (or them) with him.

OEO has found it necessary to press New Haven hard in order to broaden board membership to include representatives of the neighborhood poor.

Community action, we have seen, emerges early as the most striking new concept in President Johnson's war on poverty. And it has sufficient funds to attract the interest of mayors who do not really agree with it. In one sense, community action is an administrative concept calling for a new method of administering welfare policies. In another sense, community action is a technique for social action. And the one can hardly be separated from the other.

Community action was placed in the Economic Opportunity Act upon the recommendation of a small group of professionals who were not only interested in a better administration of existing programs, but who had definite views on the need for changing the institutions that serve the poor. They also had convictions as to the role the poor *ought to play* in bringing about those changes. Community action is not merely another administrative arrangement; it is a method of social action aimed at far-reaching social reform.

One of the principal targets the professional planners had in mind was the Negro ghetto. Title II of the Economic Opportunity Act provides an opportunity for the American Negro to transform his image of himself by using federal funds and federal standards to demand that city hall and its bureaucracies provide services for him and his family equal to those normally available for white middle-class America. In the process, if community action were to work as it was intended to work, the powerless of the city would soon be generating power of their own. Community action may have found its way into the act because the Bureau of the Budget thought it had located a new "coordinating" device, but once there it immediately became an instrument with a political potential which is incalculable.

Community action, nevertheless, was placed in the act and given major status without any significant pressure from the great interest groups and certainly without any public demand. In that sense, it is a fair example of what Glazer and Moynihan have called "the professionalism of reform," if we add the all-important proviso that the Negro crisis and President Johnson's need for his own program provided the occasion for professional ingenuity to work. At that, community action appears to have been politically more than the President probably bargained for.

As for the corollary "maximum feasible participation" of the poor, the suspicion is great that the technicians sneaked in a concept without realizing (or did they?) how profoundly they were probing the murkier depths of American urban politics. History has many ironies. It can now add another; the Johnson war on poverty incorporated wholesale a philosophy of social action which had been nurtured close to Robert Kennedy's own office. But there is a greater irony; Lyndon Johnson, seeker of consensus, one-time member of the conservative Inner Club, wittingly or unwittingly has unleashed a force which can unsettle traditional politics and greatly affect the traditional exercise of power.

CHAPTER 4

COMMUNITY ACTION
IN ACTION:
THE POLITICS OF
ADMINISTRATION

"Americans are conditioned by their history to look upon Administration as itself a branch of Government: as within 'politics.' "

GUNNAR MYRDAL,
An American Dilemma (1944).

T HE FIRST YEAR OF community action is destined to rank among the most important case studies in the field of modern public administration. It may be a long time before the full story is told, but a beginning must be made, and this study, which is more concerned with the political than the administrative implications of the Johnson war on poverty, attempts to do so. The previous chapter analyzed the "theory" of community action, especially as it developed in the thinking and planning of the professional staff of the President's Committee on Juvenile Delinquency during the Kennedy years. This chapter will follow the same central concepts—community action and "maximum feasible participation"—as they become operational realities in a multimillion-dollar program reaching literally hundreds of American communities.

The fact that community action rapidly came to have some meaning in hundreds of communities is significant in itself. One point of view which emerged in the discussions during the formulation of the Economic Opportunity Act asserted that community action ought to be applied in a limited number of large cities. There was the experience of the Ford Foundation "gray areas" program to build upon and there were some sixteen communities in which the President's Committee on Juvenile Delinquency had already placed "seed money." This school of thought inclined to the view that it would be well to make a maximum effort in perhaps ten communities having the toughest problems.

Mr. Shriver, director of the new Office of Economic Opportunity, personally came to favor a broader attack through a national program which would begin just as rapidly as possible in hundreds of communities. The director was evidently supported in this by the White House; thus, community action as an administrative and political reality almost immediately became a national phenomenon. This high-level decision *not* to limit community action to a selected and limited list of communities profoundly affected the nature of the organization Mr. Shriver's Office of Economic Opportunity was to be. It also led to a certain amount of confusion concerning OEO's role in the poverty war.[1]

OEO: FISH OR FOWL?

In one sense, by placing the Office of Economic Opportunity in the Executive Office of the President and by appointing a man of national prominence as director, the Johnson administration appeared to be creating a White House-level coordinating agency with a mandate to pull together the efforts of all relevant agencies and departments in a combined federal attack on poverty. In another sense, since it was decided early in the game that OEO should be directly responsible for administering the community action program which was to affect hundreds of communities, urban and rural, large and small, across the country, Mr. Shriver actually was assuming responsibility for a major operating program. Thus, from the very beginning of the program, Mr. Shriver's new organization has been torn between the role of overall coordinator, which would seem to call for a relatively small, elite planning group (somewhat analagous to the Bureau of the Budget with its highly competent five hundred specialists), and that of an operating agency requiring a bureaucratic staff numbering in the several thousands.

In addition to the enormous responsibilities which community action (Title II) imposes, Mr. Shriver also made it clear from the very beginning that the Job Corps was to be administered directly out of his office. This again was a key decision with the greatest possible implications for the kind of administrative structure which the Office of Economic Opportunity was to become. The Job Corps was a major operating program—in some ways as complex and as difficult as community action—and yet it was to be administered from the level of the Executive Office of the President. OEO also immediately took responsibility for VISTA, a kind of domestic peace corps.

The fish or fowl dilemma has plagued OEO from that day forward. A White House agency may try coordinating the overlapping programs of executive departments and agencies. As soon as it undertakes operating programs of its own and comes into conflict with other operating programs, it will have to be coordinated by someone else, quite possibly the Bureau of the Budget.

Actually, Mr. Shriver's official life has been even more complicated than this brief summary suggests. The President, for reasons that have always been obscure, kept Mr. Shriver for many months as director of the Peace Corps as well as director of the inherently bifurcated OEO. In addition to this, various parts of the Economic Opportunity Act were negotiated away to the various operating departments—most notably the Department of Labor and the Department of Health, Education, and Welfare—for purposes of administration. Thus Title IB, which makes possible a national program of work-training for young people, was delegated immediately to the Secretary of Labor who established a Neighborhood Youth Corps as part of that department's new Manpower Administration. In terms of the number of youths served, the Neighborhood Youth Corps soon became the largest single youth program in the antipoverty program. Likewise Title IC, which provides for a work-study program for college students, was delegated a year later to the Office of Education for administrative purposes. Title V, which provides for a program of training for heads of households who have been on relief, was delegated immediately to the Department of Health, Education, and Welfare.

Two years after the program was launched, Mr. Shriver had to defend himself against charges that the antipoverty program was an "administrative shambles." His defense was that if it were an administrative shambles, he was proud to be in charge.[2] A better defense would have been that if it were *not* an administrative shambles he and his associates in OEO had performed a modern miracle. To conceive a new multimillion-dollar national program which is to be administered in part by a White House-level co-ordinating agency and in part by operating departments, and which at the same time is to be coordinated by some new White House office which itself becomes part of the administrative overlap, is to postulate administrative chaos. Only a nation as gifted as we are in organizational talent would risk launching a promising new program in such a highly disadvantageous administrative setting.

Mr. Shriver also faced the problem which any new agency head faces of finding a competent staff, including high-powered associates, gifted enough to want to take on the administrative and political headaches of complex operating programs such as community action and the Job Corps. In this connection, the loss of Adam Yarmolinsky in August was a serious blow. Indeed, it might have been critical but for Shriver's good fortune in having acquired previously the services of Jack Conway, long-time assistant to Walter Reuther. Mr. Conway who was on leave from his position as executive director of the Industrial Union Department of the AFL-CIO had been working with the Shriver task force since March and was responsible for developing the community action program. Although Conway had expressed his personal desire to return to his trade-union position at an early date, he was willing to accept the position of deputy administrator during the initial phase in order to help get the program into operation. Conway was another key man in the Johnson poverty war who had strong Kennedy ties—having served as deputy administrator of the Housing and Home Finance Agency during the early Kennedy years. Conway's previous experience indicated that he would bring to the OEO deputy position a combination of administrative ability, political sophistication, and, not least important, a sense of how to move within the confines of the bureaucratic maze which pervades official Washington. Conway's principal assignment was one that he liked, to get Title II (community action) into operation *in as many communities as possible, as soon as possible.* Conway's right-hand man in this undertaking was Richard Boone, a young professional from the staff of the President's Committee on Juvenile Delinquency who had previously worked for the Ford Foundation.

Time was of the essence. Although the appropriation for the war on poverty was through Congress by October 3, 1964, a high-level decision held up the funding of any specific projects until after the presidential election (a rather handsomely non-political gesture from the Johnson White House). The first projects were announced by Mr. Shriver on November 25. Hence, the largest single problem Mr. Shriver and Mr. Conway faced was to find worthy projects for $800 million between November 25 and June 30, 1965, the end of the fiscal year. The first year of the war on poverty, in fact, was telescoped into about six and a half months of administrative action.

SHRIVER FACES CONGRESS: ROUND ONE

The second most immediate problem facing OEO in mid-November, 1964, was having something to say to the Congress shortly after the first of the year. Only experienced Washington hands and a few specialists in the federal budgetary process will realize that the executive budget for the next fiscal year (in this case, beginning on July 1, 1965), starts taking final form by mid-November of the previous year. Mr. Shriver did not have anything more than a skeleton organization in November, 1964. He had the problem of disbursing $800 million in hundreds of local communities in a period of about six months. Yet, in half that time, Shriver would be facing congressional committees, asking for more money for another year and answering questions about how his new program was going. And during the period from mid-November to mid-December, 1964, the embryonic Shriver office had to make basic budget decisions about the shape and scope of their massive program which was yet to be seen in operation.

One does not exaggerate the problem in stating it in this fashion. Actually, Mr. Shriver testified before a House subcommittee on April 2, 1965, about the new program. Was Congress likely to be curious about the results of the new program before there could possibly be any results? Or was Congress willing to defer a close examination until the following year—1966—by which time presumably there would be enough administrative experience to offer a basis for judgment?

If he took time to glance back, Mr. Shriver must have remembered that the program moved through the Congress with relative ease in 1964; only in the appropriations committees was there anything resembling a hard look, and in that case the billion-dollar program was trimmed to eight hundred million by a rule of thumb, because OEO would have less than twelve months in which to put the program into effect. Looking ahead to 1965, Shriver found himself in a situation in which his new program would be under review in Congress before there could be any administrative results worth examining. Hence, there was the distinct possibility that the Johnson antipoverty program would be given virtually a free ride through another session of Congress.

This is approximately what happened in 1965. The Republicans who felt they had been bluntly turned aside in 1964 might be ignored with impunity now that President Johnson had been to the polls in November and had won a landslide victory in his own right. In the process, the LBJ coattails carried into Congress the largest Democratic majorities since the days of FDR. The Johnson landslide added forty-two new Democratic seats in the House. Once again we encounter basic legislative arithmetic. Since each vote counts double (add one Democrat, subtract one Republican), the strongest president since Roosevelt had acquired a plus eighty-four advantage in the House of Representatives in the Eighty-ninth Congress.

What this meant for the poverty program was that any effective critique would have to come from administration Democrats in the Congress, and it was fairly predictable that administration loyalists would not go out of their way to give the war on poverty a hard time during its first year of operation. It was after all only a six-month-old infant. Any significant congressional review of the antipoverty program would have to wait at least until 1966.

In the meantime, OEO experienced no shortage of administrative problems; a good many of them soon revealed themselves to be political problems as well.

THE MAYORS REACT

Community action was hardly underway before the first signs of resistance were felt. They came with increasing intensity from San Francisco all the way to New York City. John F. Shelley, Democratic mayor of San Francisco, charged that OEO was "undermining the integrity of local government" by organizing the poor into militant, politically active groups. Mayor Shelley was candid in his insistence that the "elected city official must retain control." By June of the first year, Shelley and Mayor Samuel Yorty of Los Angeles (another Democrat) sponsored a resolution at the U.S. Conference of Mayors accusing Sargent Shriver of "fostering class struggle." Democratic Mayor Wagner of New York told a House subcommittee, "I feel very strongly that the sovereign part of each locality . . . should have the power of approval over the makeup of the planning group, over the structure of the planning group, over the plan."[3]

What seemed to be causing the greatest difficulty was Section 202 (a) (3) of the act which defines a community action program as one which ". . . is developed, conducted, and administered with the maximum feasible participation of residents of the areas and members of the groups served." We recall that this section was the creature of the staff of the President's Committee on Juvenile Delinquency and that it received very little attention from the committees of Congress in 1964.

Section 202 (a) (3) was not being overlooked or neglected in the development of OEO's national program. As early as February, 1965, OEO issued a community action program guide to be used by local communities which stated: "A vital feature of every community action program is the involvement of the poor themselves—the residents of the areas and members of the groups to be served—in planning, policy-making, and operation of the program."

The same program guide clarified the meaning of "maximum feasible participation": the poor were to participate "either on the governing body or on a policy advisory committee," or to have "at least one representative selected from each of the neighborhoods" involved in the program.

The guide went one step further and recommended elections among the poor to fill these positions "whenever feasible." The guide did not state, but it was widely understood, that OEO was using a rule-of-thumb standard requiring that one-third of the local poverty board members were to be drawn from the poor.

No matter how seriously the Office of Economic Opportunity

intended its administrative policy to be taken at the local level, one can imagine that the national director of the program, Mr. Shriver, would prefer having some flexibility of action on the troublesome issue of representation of the poor. It is one thing to insist on the one-third ratio in Portland, Maine, where there is no mayor, weak or strong, and no boiling dark ghetto; but it is quite another thing in Mayor Richard Daley's Chicago with its powerful Democratic political machine and the nation's largest Negro ghetto. The student of American public administration realizes that this was not the first time that an unsettling (and unsettled) new policy had to be adjusted a little bit this way, a little bit that way as the pressures shifted and mounted.

The pressures mounted and the policy adjusted and shifted. Atlanta, Georgia, developed a community action program which soon became Mr. Shriver's pride and joy; yet the poor were conspicuously absent from its board. Newark, New Jersey, at the other extreme, established a board from which city hall was virtually excluded. OEO was reluctant to take on Mayor Daley in Chicago; it courageously struggled with Mayor Shelley in San Francisco. All through the months of 1965, Sargent Shriver resembled nothing so much as a skilled tightrope walker as he moved with a certain nimbleness of tread.

In Miami Beach on August 11, Mr. Shriver denied that his agency had set arbitrary quotas for representation of the poor; he also explained that representatives of the poor did not have to be poor themselves. A week later, Mayor Yorty of Los Angeles publicly blasted Shriver, accusing him of cutting off federal funds as a means of forcing Los Angeles to increase the number of poor people in the planning process. A month later, at a ceremony celebrating an additional grant of funds to Atlanta, Mr. Shriver praised the local antipoverty program as a "shining example." On this occasion, under questioning from a newsman, Mr. Shriver was careful to explain that the involvement of the poor in policy-making was an evolutionary process.

Pressure from the mayors mounted steadily. At the annual meeting of the U.S. Conference of Mayors in June, the mayors' executive committee approved a resolution urging that OEO recognize existing or city hall-endorsed local agencies as the proper channel for community action projects. The mayors formed a new antipoverty committee with Mayor Daley of Chicago as chairman.

The selection of Mayor Daley would have special meaning in Washington where it already seemed to be well understood that *no* antipoverty programs were to be set up in Chicago except through city hall. Mayor Daley and his committee lost no time meeting with Vice-President Humphrey (*not* with Mr. Shriver) and Theodore Berry, who was the man directly responsible for community action in the rapidly expanding OEO headquarters staff. The mayors expressed concern over OEO's tendency to support community action projects which were independent of city hall. According to John Gunther, executive director of the Conference of Mayors, the Vice-President told the mayors' antipoverty committee the Johnson administration intended to work closely with the mayors. In August Vice-President Humphrey addressed the National League of Cities: "I can tell you now that your important role is assured in this program. I'm your built-in Special Agent to make sure that you are represented in this program twenty four hours a day, 365 days a year. I've been hired for you."[4] These words coming from a former mayor must have been especially reassuring to the current crop of mayors.

CITIZENS CRUSADE:
THE VOICE OF CONSCIENCE

In September, 1965, Jack Conway left his position as deputy to Sargent Shriver and returned to his position as executive director of the Industrial Union Department of the AFL-CIO. At almost the same point of time, it was announced that a new group, the Citizens' Crusade Against Poverty, was to be formed, and that Mr. Conway would be prominently involved in its activities. Mr. Conway took with him from OEO to serve as director of the Citizens Crusade Richard Boone, the former JD committee staff man who had helped write the concept "maximum feasible participation" of the poor into the Act and into OEO administrative practice. The Citizens Crusade Against Poverty, a private organization, was chaired by Walter Reuther; its members included individuals prominent in civic, civil rights, church, and liberal organizations; finances were supplied by the United Auto Workers and by the Ford Foundation. Those close to the new organization hoped it might become the "conscience" of the antipoverty program. The position of deputy to Mr. Shriver was now taken by Bernard L.

Boutin, a Democrat from New Hampshire who had served throughout the Kennedy years as administrator of the General Services
Administration. Mr. Boutin was appointed deputy director of OEO
on October 21, 1965, reasonably close to the first anniversary of
the antipoverty program. Mr. Boutin, who had once served as
Mayor of Laconia, New Hampshire, arrived on the OEO scene
amidst growing rumors and newspaper reports that the Johnson
administration was disenchanted with the political repercussions
of community action programs in big cities.

On November 5, 1965, Joseph Loftus reported in the *New York
Times* that the Bureau of the Budget had told the Office of Economic Opportunity that it would prefer less emphasis on policy-
making by the poor in planning community action projects. The
story continued:

> Maximum feasible participation by the poor in the antipoverty
> program is called for by the law. In the Bureau's view this
> means primarily using the poor to carry out the program but
> not to design it. This viewpoint was acknowledged today by a
> high government source who refused to be identified.

Someone was talking out of school—or was he?

It requires little imagination to realize how rapidly this story
spread to every city hall and to a great many poor neighborhoods
in America. Mr. Shriver, who was delivering an address in Scotts-
dale, Arizona, when the story broke, issued an immediate denial
which Mr. Loftus carefully reported in the *Times* the next morning.
"Unfortunately," said Mr. Shriver, "the article gives the impression
that the Bureau of the Budget's 'alleged' position is official government policy that is about to be implemented by OEO." "Moreover," he continued, "it seems to imply that such a policy has been
enunciated by the White House. Frankly, no such change in OEO's
policy has been directed or ordered by anyone in the Administration. Our policy is today and will remain exactly what it has been
from the very beginning."

Perhaps this strong statement from Mr. Shriver helped clear the
air, assuming that all concerned understood what OEO's policy
had been from the beginning. On the other hand, if Mr. Shriver
had wished to keep some degree of administrative flexibility, he
was now more firmly committed than ever to "maximum feasible
participation" of the poor—or so at least it seemed late in 1965.

In the present case, the policy was made, in a sense, when the original task force put the concept "maximum feasible participation" in Title II of the proposed bill. Congress helped to harden the policy decision when it endorsed (albeit uncritically) the concept which remained in Title II of the Economic Opportunity Act of 1964. But Congress did not read substance into the words, and so it was left to Mr. Shriver, whose office assumed responsibility for administering Title II, to determine what "maximum feasible participation" was to mean in Chicago, in New Haven, in Portland, in San Francisco, in Atlanta, and in hundreds of other American communities.

ENTER THE BUREAU OF THE BUDGET

Yet a curious thing has occurred. The Bureau of the Budget, an elite organization of about five hundred career civil servants (only the director is appointed by the president), able and hard-working men, but not members of this or of any political administration, appears to have a different view from Mr. Shriver, who is a presidential appointee and the man responsible for the program. And the difference is not over a procedural matter—this is not a matter of mechanical routine. The issue is basic to the war on poverty; it is a policy issue, and it has direct, immediate, and profound *political* implications. The picture one gets does not fit easily the commonly held notion that elected political officials make public policy while career civil servants are there to carry out the policy.

Of course it is possible to conjecture that the Bureau of the Budget was simply moving in the direction that the President wanted to move. But this is not a very comforting thought. It suggests that the Bureau of the Budget knew better than Sargent Shriver how the President wished to have the war on poverty conducted (we have noted that Mr. Shriver was most emphatic in denying that the bureau's position had White House authority behind it). If the bureau was being used to apply a White House curb, it had the odd immediate result of pinning Mr. Shriver publicly to the "hard-line" position on "maximum feasible participation."

The result at the local level was a fair amount of confusion in the mind of any responsible local poverty warrior trying to understand what "maximum feasible participation" of the poor ought to mean in his community in order to make it eligible for federal funds.

What does the antipoverty program do to the pattern of federal-local relationships? There can be no doubt that the Economic Opportunity Act and the antipoverty programs it sponsors have brought Washington and city hall into direct contact in a new and strikingly different way. One of the most interesting aspects of the new legislation is its heavy reliance on local initiative. Even more interesting and significant, however, is the potential for conflict between the federal government and the local political power structure which is provided in the words which specify that there shall be "maximum feasible participation" of residents of the areas and members of the groups served. These words may very well indicate the most significant social welfare innovation since the days of the New Deal. The words, also, have great political significance, great political potential. Neighborhood participation on the part of poor people has already encouraged some to undertake the task of organizing the poor politically. The Saul Alinsky school has been at work in Chicago, Rochester, Syracuse, and possibly elsewhere. The Alinsky point of view holds that with political power, the poor in America may be able to bring about a social revolution against the entrenched establishment. Alinsky argues that poor people will never get what they want and need until they learn to grasp the levers of local political power. Little wonder that the occupants of city hall are nervous. It would be a serious error, however, to assume that the political potential here has only local significance.[5]

Consider for a moment the nature of our great national presidential elections, specifically the contest between Senator Kennedy and Vice-President Nixon in 1960. In that election almost sixty-nine million Americans voted. The two candidates were separated at the end by only about one hundred thousand votes. Kennedy received 49.7 per cent of the total vote; the Nixon percentage was 49.6. One-tenth of one per cent separated the two candidates in our great contest. The photo-finish of 1960 was a little unusual, but American presidential elections (1964 being aberrational) tend to be remarkably close. Yet when one examines the 1960 election, he discovers that although sixty-nine million Americans voted, another forty million adult Americans did not participate even to the extent of voting. This is normal also.

An increasing body of empirical data about American voting and participation in politics indicates that political apathy has its greatest incidence among people of low economic and social status. A set of programs which might stimulate a sense of political concern and political involvement among the poor of our blighted urban neighborhoods could have the most profound implications for the future of American politics.

There is, indeed, a school of thought in American political science, for example, which suggests that the great stability, the great sense of concord, in our American political system rests essentially on the fact that there are millions of Americans who are politically apathetic and who are not drawn into the political process in any contentious or unsettling way.

Professor E. E. Schattschneider observed:

> The whole balance of power in the political system could be overturned by a massive invasion of the political system, and nothing tangible protects the system against the flood. All that is necessary to produce the most painless revolution in history, the first revolution ever legalized in advance, is to have a sufficient number of people do something not much more difficult than to walk across the street on election day.[6]

President Johnson's declaration of war on poverty may have been a supremely political act on the part of a supremely political man. If so, community action appears to be a concept conceived by a small group of experts in a limited field of specialization. They undoubtedly were encouraged in their efforts by Attorney-General Robert Kennedy. "Maximum feasible participation" of the poor is almost certainly a concept which is in the Act because the technicians put it there. But the concept when applied in the administration of the program soon achieves a strong political punch. The mayors react; the administrators vacillate; and suddenly the politically troublesome administrative concept is toned down by another group of professionals in the Bureau of the Budget. It seems very strange behavior in an administration which is often thought to be unusually skilled in the art of politics.

CHAPTER 5

1966—YEAR OF CRISIS

". . . the poor resist the sporadic and often patronizing attempts to draw them into a community for the very good reason that their style of life makes it impossible for them to become a part of the customary social apparatus. The prerequisites for sharing in middle class organizational life are jobs, baby sitters, and freedom from the health and housing problems that continually put the poor out of commission. A community institution requires stability and permanence for its people. . . .

"The poor don't even have a unity of their own. Those who manage to escape the condition of poverty rarely look back, and those at the bottom of the heap live in almost total isolation of each other."

JOSEPH P. LYFORD,
The Airtight Cage (1966).

THE YEAR 1966 proved difficult for President Johnson, Sargent Shriver, and the war on poverty. Before 1966 got underway, it was as certain as anything can be that Congress, acting through both its appropriations and substantive committees, would subject the antipoverty program to an infinitely more detailed legislative review than it received in either 1964 or 1965. On the other hand, it probably would not have been possible to predict just how far the legislative tightening process would go, since this was subject to influence by people and events not always part of the legislative process. In addition to a growing disposition on the part of Congress to play its traditional role of legislative overseer, the Office of Economic Opportunity now encountered strong resistance to the expansion of its programs *within* the Executive Office of the President before the program was submitted to the Congress.

The steady escalation of the war in Vietnam, and the large increase in defense expenditures which resulted from it, brought forth policy directives from the White House and the Bureau of the Budget which called for holding the line on domestic programs. There were also increasing signs—though small and relatively inconspicuous at first—of the steady erosion of President Johnson's popular and legislative support, culminating in a November off-year election which was a disaster for Great Society programs. In addition, the political-administrative strife which was present in OEO throughout 1965 gradually developed a momentum of its own in 1966, until it threatened to tear the agency—and the program—apart.

OMENS OF TROUBLE

Ill omens appeared just before Christmas, 1965, as "informed sources" advised Eve Edstrom of the *Washington Post* that the Bureau of the Budget was prepared to cut the Office of Economic Opportunity requests for funds in the coming fiscal year from $2.5 billion to about $1.5 billion. While it is normal for the Bureau of the Budget to trim the requests of operating agencies, the proportions suggested in this case were clearly excessive *if* the administration intended even a slight escalation of its war against poverty. The final figure requested by the administration in its budget message to Congress was $1.75 billion, a figure plausible enough to stifle widespread criticism outside government yet sufficiently restrictive to cause considerable dismay in OEO headquarters. The reasons for the dismay were not trivial.

We recall that the antipoverty program began late in 1964 with an $800 million program, but this was for the first eight months of operation. For the next fiscal year running from July 1, 1965, to June 30, 1966, Congress appropriated $1.5 billion. In its budget proposal for the next fiscal year, terminating on June 30, 1967, the Johnson administration was asking for $1.75 billion. This would include all OEO activities: community action and its healthy offspring, Project Head Start, the Job Corps, the Neighborhood Youth Corps, VISTA, Work-Study, Work Experience. While 1.75 billion is transparently a larger sum than 1.5 billion, simple arithmetic can sometimes be misleading in the esoteric field of federal budgeting. In *rate of spending,* the Johnson administration was actually proposing a somewhat smaller program in fiscal 1967. The financial details are intricate, but in essence, by the spring of 1966, Mr. Shriver's office was funding projects *at a rate* higher than they would be able to maintain throughout the next fiscal year under the $1.75 billion ceiling which the Administration placed on OEO program activity early in 1966.[1]

Although, for obvious reasons, it was not a matter of great public discussion at the time, during the battle of the budget which took place within the White House in December and January, the war on poverty became the first domestic casualty of the war in Vietnam. Mr. Shriver's staff was justifiably concerned about the budgetary ceiling because they knew how high the level of expectations was in the local communities. No one had ever accused Mr. Shriver of underselling the potential of his program. There was now the necessity of reducing the tempo of the program, and the psychological impact on scores of communities was bound to be severe; in some cases, the slow-down might easily prove disastrous.

The budgetary limits which the White House imposed early in 1966 came at a time when the top administrative structure in OEO was in a state of extreme flux. Jack Conway left his position as Shriver's chief deputy in September, 1965, to return to his labor-union post (and to a new role in the Citizens Crusade Against Poverty). Richard Boone, community action expert, went with him. Bernard Boutin was handpicked by the White House to replace Conway early in October, 1965. Boutin served in OEO only eight months. His relations with Shriver apparently were not very effective, and on May 8, 1966, the President appointed Mr. Boutin to the position of administrator of the Small Business Administration.

It was not only the deputy position which proved troublesome. Within a period of a few months, Mr. Shriver lost the services of Holmes Brown, assistant director for public affairs, who returned to private industry; William Haddad, assistant director for inspection, who returned to New York City; Gillis Long, a former member of Congress who had been in charge of congressional relations; and Otis Singletarry, Job Corps director, who returned to the University of North Carolina. Although Shriver was able in time to find competent replacements, the rapid turnover among so many key men added to the tension within OEO early in 1966.

On the other hand, Mr. Shriver began another year with convincing evidence that he had the continuing support of the President. A White House task force which had been examining the role of the proposed Department of Urban Affairs recommended in January that the community action program be moved from OEO to the new department. Whatever administrative logic there may have been in the recommendation, the loss would have been devastating not only to OEO's prestige but more importantly to its "sense of mission." Devoted community action professionals in OEO were convinced, moreover, that a transfer to the new department would stifle a program which had already produced strong counter political pressures from the mayors. It must have been especially reassuring to Mr. Shriver and his closest associates, therefore, to have the President side with Shriver in a major behind-the-scenes bureaucratic struggle.

So community action was to stay put, at least for the time being. But real damage had been done. For the first time since OEO was created in 1964, the major newspapers of the country carried authoritative and remarkably detailed accounts of major "bureaucratic" problems and struggles within a Shriver-led organization. The legend that Mr. Shriver was somehow immune to the difficulties which plague other public administrators grew tarnished. The aura of success surrounding the Peace Corps did not carry over to the new program.

One report had it that Jack Conway who had been the strong community action proponent within OEO was now leading an attempt to move community action to the new department. Conway had served as deputy administrator of the Housing and Home Finance Agency (destined to form the nucleus of any new urban affairs department) during the Kennedy years, and hence his views might very well be influential with the White House task force.[2]

COMMITTEE DISENCHANTMENT

Mr. Shriver also encountered a changed mood toward his program on Capitol Hill. This was a new experience for Shriver who had shown an unusual talent for mollifying congressional critics. From the outset of the committee hearings in March, 1966, it was perfectly clear that Congress was ready to place specific statutory restrictions on several aspects of the antipoverty program. The difference in mood was partially attributable to the fact that a House subcommittee had spent much of the autumn of 1965 looking into antipoverty projects in several cities across the country. Consequently, when Sargent Shriver went before the House Subcommittee on Education and Labor in the spring of 1966, he faced a group of congressmen who had some first-hand impressions of their own about the progress of the war on poverty. In the Senate, the tightening-up process actually started in November of the previous year. A Senate appropriations subcommittee had undertaken its own investigation, but this was limited to one particular project, a Head Start grant in Mississippi. The Mississippi episode merits full examination in the next chapter, but in view of the congressional critique of 1966, it should be noted here that the Senate, through its Appropriations Committee, tightened its controls on OEO as early as November, 1965.[3]

Thus, Sargent Shriver appeared before Congressman Powell's House Education and Labor Subcommittee in 1966 in a spirit of compromise. Shriver was prepared to accept mild reform proposals as a means of heading off any more drastic shakeup of his program. The *Wall Street Journal* (March 9, 1966) accurately summarized Shriver's position:

> To quiet Democratic complaints about relatively unsupervised local projects, Mr. Shriver proposed tighter Federal direction of "community action" agencies, which would be required to submit to regular Federal audits and evaluations. Washington would also supervise their hiring and pay policies and an identification with partisan political activities would be prohibited.
>
> To put a clamp on local staffs and salaries . . . Mr. Shriver agreed privately to a provision limiting administrative expenses to 10% of any "community action" budget.

On the other hand, Shriver was firm in resisting the Republican suggestion that Head Start, or any other program, should be separated from OEO and assigned to other federal agencies or departments.

Testifying on March 8, Sargent Shriver informed the House committee that 2,200,000 Americans had moved out of the poverty bracket in 1965, leaving thirty-two million fellow citizens still in a condition of poverty. Thanks to a healthy and booming economy, ". . . the economic well being of most Americans and the overall poverty situation are improving," he continued, "but the remaining poor are being dragged down. Concentrated. Backed into corners like the Delta and like Watts. It is the needs of these people to which our programs are directed."

Two days later, Representative Quie, Republican of Minnesota, questioned Mr. Shriver rather sharply on the involvement of the poor. The lack of a clear-cut OEO guideline on the participation issue apparently disturbed the Congressman. Representative Quie was concerned about frequently changing interpretations and regulations having to do with the representation of poor people on local community action boards. He pointed to the difference between Chicago, with only token representation of the poor, and San Francisco, where he found authentic representation of poor people at the policy-making level. "This constant difference," he said, "and . . . vacillation in the program that we see all over the country is, I think, one of the reasons for the tremendous controversy."

Mr. Shriver's response was that the great variety in types of local programs and in the types of problems faced by local communities required a flexible program, not one which consisted of rigidly established and executed standards. "Instead of trying to make all of these rigid rules in Washington," Shriver continued,

> we have been trying to mold this program to the needs of the localities on the theory that this is a local community action program. It is not a Federal program where all of the rules are made in Washington, and everybody has to get lockstep into line with the Federal Government. . . . We are trying to put this program into the hands of local people.

But the Congressman wanted to know why community action funds had been given in the first place to community action boards which obviously reflected little or no representation of the poor. Mr. Shriver's answer was that OEO was constantly working to achieve broader local representation. "We don't expect to have everything perfect right off the bat, but we don't expect, on the other hand, people to do nothing, no genuine effort to make the committees broadly representative and to involve minority groups."

Finally, Mr. Quie asked whether Mr. Shriver would favor a specific statutory requirement that one-third of any community action board be representatives of the poor. Mr. Shriver replied,

> Rigid requirements established here in Washington do not conform in many cases to the realities of situations around the country. We work together for it [participation of the poor], I

think, better than when we, as policemen, have a speed limit, a slow limit, and rigidly enforce it with a blackjack.[4]

THE POOR SPEAK OUT

In addition to the gradual tightening of administrative and legislative controls on the program, Shriver had a dramatic face-to-face encounter with militant spokesmen for the urban poor, some of whom, he soon discovered, held the program in contempt. The occasion was a national convention of poverty warriors which convened in Washington in the middle of April. Walter Reuther, chairman of the conference's principal sponsoring group, the Citizens Crusade Against Poverty, described the convention as representing the "broadest coalition of concerned citizens ever to be gathered in the Nation's Capital." The aims of the Crusade's first convention were outlined by Richard Boone, formerly a leading draftsman of community action within OEO and now the executive director of the Crusade:

> First, and more importantly, to marshal forces that will guarantee the poor equal power in the war on poverty.
>
> Second, to encourage the Federal Government to seek new ways to support actively the local groups representing the poor.
>
> Third, to challenge private agencies all over the land to seek new ways to support directly the grass-roots organizations of the poor.
>
> Fourth, to bring forth new national programs and policies to speed up the war on poverty.[5]

Speakers at the convention included Mr. Reuther, whose union had contributed one million dollars to the Crusade; Roy Wilkins, executive director of the NAACP; Dr. Eugene Carson Blake, secretary-elect of the World Council of Churches; and Mr. Shriver. Participants included Bayard Rustin, Leon Keyserling, and Rabbi Richard Hirsch.

The list of participants also included Mrs. Unita Blackwell from the Mississippi Delta who declared: "Help us catch up—if you don't we'll run off and leave you." Her plea that the "time is now" to make a new beginning in the war on poverty provoked standing applause from the one thousand delegates. Mrs. Blackwell said that OEO should be ashamed of itself, that it was condoning hand-picked antipoverty boards in Mississippi which put the war on poverty in the hands of police chiefs who beat Negroes and mayors who deprive people of their rights.

"They are going to see about my poverty," she said. "They have *kept* me in poverty." Money, she observed, is available "quick, fast and in a hurry" when it comes to supporting the war in Vietnam. But when the poor seek funds, they are told "to draw up another proposal."[6]

When Sargent Shriver attempted to address a luncheon meeting of the convention the next day, he was booed, jostled, and almost hooted down. According to the *New York Times,*

> Mr. Shriver plunged on with his speech despite the uproar and shouts of "You're lying" and "Stop listening to him" from a rebel group that moved up near the stage. The director of OEO looking strained and upset was hustled from the International Inn immediately after his speech despite pleas to remain for questions. "I will not participate in a riot," he declared.[7]

"Nothing like this has ever happened to him," declared Herbert J. Kramer, Mr. Shriver's public affairs director. Bayard Rustin explained that when ". . . people heard him describing what was happening in their own neighborhoods"—neighborhoods which they believed were untouched by the drive against poverty—they became upset. Outside the meeting hall, Jack Conway, principal organizer of the convention, said: "I don't know where we go from here. They're wrecking the meeting. They have turned on the people who wanted to help them."[8]

Bayard Rustin commented later, "This was not a spontaneous demonstration. Some of the people shouting about the poor participating were not poor but have a vested interest. And some of the members came into the meeting with a sheet that was printed up several hours before."[9]

After he had had time for reflection, Sargent Shriver told a news conference that "the people involved in the yelling business were determined beforehand upon breaking up the meeting as an end in itself."

Mr. Shriver rejected the view that his speech triggered the protest or that the demonstration stemmed from widespread dissatisfaction with the antipoverty program. He suggested that a large number of the discontented also were those who were opposed to American involvement in Vietnam. The protesters, he continued, had an "anti-establishment" bias and tended to view the Crusade's convention as an "establishment" meeting; the poor who attended were angry because they had no representation on the Crusade's distinguished board of directors.

Not so, retorted Jack Conway, Shriver's former deputy; "Shriver was trying to overwhelm them with success statistics. They released their anger and deepest frustrations at not seeing results."[10]

Perhaps the most plausible explanation of what occurred is that a poor people's convention, organized by Reuther, Conway, Boone, *et al.* presumably to exert pressure on the administration to intensify its antipoverty efforts, provided a unique opportunity for a new indigenous militancy to express itself. And express itself it did, beyond the expectations of the convention planners. It was disingenuous of Sargent Shriver to suggest that the anger was not directed at him and his program. But the episode also illuminates the widening chasm which separates the spokesmen of the New Left from the established civil rights and labor leaders. Bayard Rustin, organizer of the March on Washington in August, 1963, appears a little awkward in attempting to explain the incident without revealing that he no longer speaks for the new militancy. Nor was Shriver completely wrong in his ironic observation that a Crusade led by Walter Reuther and Dr. Eugene Carson Blake does indeed carry the establishment image, so far as many young people who are impoverished and alienated are concerned.[11]

THE STRINGS TIGHTEN

Back on Capitol Hill, the House Committee on Education and Labor had completed hearings on the program on March 23. It was authoritatively reported late in April that Democrats on the committee had been holding secret caucuses and were about to confront their Republican committee colleagues with a Democratic consensus. For the first time since the inception of the program, committee Democrats were believed ready to limit community action funds and were prepared to place a good many specific restrictions on Shriver's administration of the program. One anonymous House Democrat said that the "participation of the poor" issue had stimulated "ugly problems of the political establishment." "Extremist groups," he darkly observed, "have seized it as a forum for dissent."[12]

When the House committee reported the bill (HR 15111) in mid-May, the administration was undoubtedly pleased that the amount authorized—$1.75 billion—coincided with the President's request. Apart from total dollars, the administration could find little basis for satisfaction in the work of the House committee which made significant changes in the allocation of funds and, even more importantly, in the structure and administration of several OEO programs.

Some of the more important changes were:

1. Community action was to receive $805 million, but the committee specified how all but $323 million was to be spent.

2. At least twenty per cent of all community action funds were to be used for programs funded independently of city-wide community action agencies.

3. Eighty-eight million dollars of community action funds were earmarked specifically for a new program of public service employment for hard-core unemployed adults.

4. A new program for prevention and treatment of drug addiction was to receive $12.5 million of community action money.

5. At least $352 million of community action money was to go into the Head Start program.

6. Another $22 million of community action money was to provide legal services for the poor.

7. A limit of $12,500 was placed on the federal contribution to annual salary of any local poverty official.

8. The Job Corps was limited to an enrollment of forty-five thousand, of whom ten thousand were to be women.

While the action of the House committee caused real anxiety within OEO, the publicity given a report by a "confidential" White House task force which had been examining the administration of the poverty program left the internal difficulties of the Shriver office almost indecently exposed to public view. The task force report implied that the effectiveness of antipoverty programs was in jeopardy because key administrative decisions had repeatedly been avoided. Press accounts in mid-May indicated that the two-hundred-page report of OEO administrative practices carried more than one hundred specific recommendations, the central finding being that OEO tended to make decisions on a case-by-case basis, developing improvised policies to deal with specific "crisis" situations after they had become public issues. The task force reportedly concluded that the administration of the program had drifted away from the original concept that antipoverty tools were to be tested in certain communities and those that held a promise of success were to have widespread application. Another major area of concern was the alleged failure of the agency to coordinate all federal programs aimed at helping the poor.[13]

As critical as the report was of OEO administrative practice, it was said to praise Sargent Shriver for an excellent job in getting a variety of complex new programs off the ground in less than two years. Nevertheless, the general thrust of the task force report seemed to be that the time had arrived for the antipoverty program to adopt the methods of "administrative management" as those techniques are generally understood throughout the federal government. In effect, the decision to move toward a system of regularized bureaucratic controls was made early in May when Bernard Boutin, deputy administrator of OEO, was given a presidential "lateral transfer" to head the Small Business Administration. The man chosen to succeed Boutin as Sargent Shriver's new chief deputy was Bertrand M. Harding, deputy commissioner of the Internal Revenue Service, a career civil servant with no background in fighting poverty but with a long career in what federal civil servants refer to as "administrative management." If it seems curious to select an Internal Revenue Service management specialist to serve as Sargent Shriver's chief-of-staff in a war on poverty, it is worth noting that Mr. Harding served as chairman of the confidential task force which had just submitted its report to the White House detailing the administrative weaknesses in Shriver's agency.

Thus the Shriver-led war on poverty after only about a year and a half of actual operation reached that point where the normal process of congressional review began to tighten legislative control of administrative action, while at the same time those forces within the executive branch which seek "coordination," "clear-cut policies," and "sound administrative practices" were spinning their web of detailed procedures and restrictions. To be sure, the process of legislative and administrative control is an inexorable one in modern government, and the Shriver program had been relatively free of these controls during the first eighteen months. Nevertheless, it is a fair question whether the manner in which Mr. Shriver ran the program did not leave it unusually vulnerable to the bureaucratic tightening process when the time came. The tragedy is that the controls were tightened at precisely the worst moment in terms of the external problems with which OEO was struggling in 1966. If one may judge by the angry voices heard at the poor people's convention in April, community action needed *more* administrative flexibility, not less, if it were to reach the desperately poor. What the war on poverty needed in 1966 was not a manual on how to write better contracts with community action agencies, but a leadership willing to say publicly that there are no easy victories, that the war on poverty, at least as much as the war in Vietnam, is expensive, and that battles will be lost, dollars wasted, and casualties suffered. The year 1966 is bound to be recorded as one in which the executive began to lose control of the war on poverty as Congress reasserted its prerogatives.

Part of the difficulty was that increasingly the White House displayed a reluctance to take on any antipoverty issue that was tough. There appears to have been a reason for the equivocal role the White House came to play. When the time of crisis arrived for OEO, the only strong group outside government prepared to do battle for the program was the Citizens Crusade. The AFL-CIO Executive Council was considerably more concerned about the repeal of Section 14b of the Taft-Hartley Law than it was about maximizing the participation of the poor. The civil rights groups were undecided about their direction after the Watts rebellion—as was revealed in the grotesque controversy which followed in the wake of the so-called Moynihan report on the Negro family.*

Just as congressional involvement in the writing of the Economic Opportunity Act was minor, so was the participation of the great organized groups. The act was written in the executive branch in a manner which minimized the participation of the powerful interest groups in the process. The opposition to the bill from the Chamber of Commerce, the National Association of Manufacturers, and the American Farm Bureau Federation in 1964 appears to have been largely *pro forma*. Support for the antipoverty program from

*A matter dealt with in more detail in Chapter 8.

the AFL-CIO and from liberal church and civil rights organizations likewise was highly ritualistic. No one has yet found much evidence to suggest that the organized "liberal" groups played a vital part either in the work of the Shriver task force or in the congressional ratification of a bill put together in the Executive Office of the President. The chief lobbying force behind the Economic Opportunity Act was the White House itself.

As a matter of fact, the creation of the Citizens Crusade by Walter Reuther and other leading figures in the liberal establishment (with funds from the United Auto Workers *and* the Ford Foundation) represented an attempt to create an interest group *after the fact* which might in time come to serve as the "conscience" of the antipoverty program. The Crusade was created and directed by men who were not unmindful of the lack of effective and sustained interest in the program on the part of the usually powerful organized groups. One assumes that the public humiliation of Sargent Shriver at the poor people's convention did little to increase the Citizens Crusade's influence with OEO.

The only other organized group which displayed an active interest during the first two years of the program was the Council of Mayors which first supported, then criticized, and finally adjusted to the program when it no longer seemed to threaten its interests.

In 1966 the staunchest advocate of an expansion and toughening of Mr. Johnson's war on poverty was Senator Robert Kennedy. He was perhaps the most outspoken of all Senate liberals in his criticism of the administration's budget policy. On April 19 Senator Kennedy assailed proposed reductions in spending for education, housing, school lunches, and antipoverty projects as "unfortunate" and "disturbing." "Time after time," Senator Kennedy declared, "the cuts will be felt most by those least able to afford them—the disadvantaged, particularly the disadvantaged children, who live in the vast urban ghettos and the rural hollows of the nation."[14]

In September Senator Kennedy took the initiative in the Senate's labor committee and presented the Johnson administration an unusual opportunity for giving the antipoverty program the transfusion it badly needed without assigning responsibility to the administration for breaking its budget ceiling. The President declined to make use of the opportunity.

A HOUSE DIVIDED

Throughout the year, the contrast between the mood of the House and of the Senate with respect to the poverty program was striking. The House in both its substantive and its appropriations committees seemed determined to impose strong restrictions on the operation of the program. The Senate displayed a far greater disposition to let Mr. Shriver have broad discretion in administering OEO programs. Nevertheless, the willingness of Senator Kennedy and Senator Joseph Clark to expand the program significantly beyond the budgetary limits which the Johnson administration had imposed was a further indication that the congressional role in the war on poverty was no longer a passive one.

We have noted how far the House Committee on Education and Labor was willing to go in providing for an increased congressional direction of program in the version of HR 15111 which it ordered reported to the House on May 18. From June until late September it was difficult to judge whether the House as a whole really wanted to take action on the program. Although the House Rules Committee had reported a resolution in mid-July providing an open rule allowing eight hours of debate on the Economic Opportunity Act amendments of 1966 (HR 15111), the debate did not take place. The reasons for the delay are not entirely clear. The Rules Committee did not specify that Chairman Adam Clayton Powell of the Committee on Education and Labor should be the floor manager as he normally would. It was believed that the Rules Committee action reflected displeasure with Mr. Powell who had failed to appear before the Rules Committee to testify in behalf of the bill. In any event, on July 19 the House Democratic leadership announced a two-week postponement of floor action, originally scheduled for the next day, amidst growing rumors that the bill lacked sufficient support. It was also known, however, that some senior House Democrats were unhappy with the action of the Rules Committee, which had violated its customary procedures when it failed to recognize the chairman of the committee reporting the bill.

Equally influential in bringing about the postponement of House action on the bill was the fact that the Civil Rights Bill was scheduled for debate on Monday, July 25; hence, voting on the economic opportunity amendments would have been squeezed into a weekend in July, when the absentee rate would be abnormally high.

The summer of 1966 dragged on without any further House action on the poverty program.

The war on poverty, which had been weakened earlier in the year by the increasing cost of the war in Vietnam, was placed in serious jeopardy by a civil war which broke out among the Democratic members of the House Committee on Education and Labor in late September. The battle between a majority of the committee's Democratic members and Chairman Adam Clayton Powell appeared to involve many things: Mr. Powell's authoritarian control of the committee staff; his frequent absenteeism; and the use of committee funds for trips by the chairman and committee staff to warmer climes. But Chairman Powell's failure to get the antipoverty program extension on the House floor for debate and a vote also influenced some committee members. One of the leaders of the Democratic committee revolt against Chairman Powell was Representative Sam M. Gibbons, a young Florida moderate who had specialized in the antipoverty program during his brief tenure on the committee. Indeed, Gibbons had been chosen months before by Chairman Powell to serve as floor manager of HR 15111, a role from which Mr. Gibbons was promptly dismissed by the chairman when his leadership in the committee coup became public knowledge.

On September 22 the House Committee on Education and Labor voted 27–1 to adopt a new set of procedures which substantially altered the relationship of the chairman to the work of the committee and its several subcommittees. If the revolt led by Representative Gibbons did in fact curb the power of Chairman Powell, the Harlem Democrat nonetheless emerged poised and affable. Within a few days of the revolt, the $1.75 billion antipoverty bill was on the floor for debate and Mr. Gibbons was restored to position of floor manager. Mr. Powell said in opening the debate: "On this side, we are in complete unanimity."[15]

A LOST OPPORTUNITY

Perhaps so. Republican spokesmen were not convinced, however. Representative William Ayres of Ohio, the ranking minority member on the House committee, told the House that the antipoverty program "was conceived in politics a few months before the 1964 election and it has been mired in politics ever since."[16]

The antipoverty campaign, Congressman Ayres continued, "is a war of the politicians, by the politicians and for the politicians, with a few crumbs left for the poor." "It was planned that way," he added.

Although administration forces were strong enough to hold off a number of Republican-sponsored amendments, especially those which would have transferred administrative control of educational programs from OEO to HEW and manpower programs to the Labor Department, they were not able to stop an amendment sponsored by Representative Albert Quie requiring that at least one-third of the members of local community action boards be representatives of the poor, and that these representatives be chosen by residents of poverty areas.

Thus, for the first time the magic words "maximum feasible participation" were to be defined in the legislation and the one-third formula was to become a fixed statutory requirement.

On the same day that the House of Representatives passed HR 15111 by a roll call vote of 210–156, the Senate Labor and Public Welfare Committee reported its version of the war on poverty (S 3164) authorizing $2,496,000,000, representing a $700 million increase over the administration's budget figure. The $700 million increase was the result of an amendment sponsored by the Kennedy brothers. Equally significant was the Senate committee's action, so different from that of the House, in *not* earmarking funds by specific program activity. The House labor committee and the House itself were prepared to place as many restrictions as possible on the Office of Economic Opportunity and especially on the community action program. The Senate committee, spurred on by Robert Kennedy, wanted a much broader program with a significant increase in rate of expenditure and with no fundamental change in the administrative apparatus at the national level.

The difference in the two congressional views can be accounted for in part by the presence of Senator Joseph Clark, chairman of a Senate subcommittee which had demonstrated a long-standing, highly professional concern for manpower and employment problems. Through its own research, his committee had developed an informed approach to the problems highlighted by the war on poverty. This time Senator Clark was joined by Senators Robert and Edward Kennedy in the drive to expand the poverty program.

The effort led by Clark and the Kennedys to expand the war on poverty and to leave a large measure of administrative control and discretion in the hands of Sargent Shriver seems to have been highly untypical of the prevailing congressional mood in 1966. The Senate readily accepted an amendment introduced by Senator Dirksen, the minority leader, which trimmed the authorization figure back to $1.75 billion, the sum suggested by the House and requested by the administration in January. Senator Dirksen took obvious delight in depicting the President as gravely concerned about congressional spending. "He fulminated like Hurricane Inez about what we were doing to his budget," the minority leader told his Senate colleagues.[17]

After three days of debate, the Senate passed HR 15111 by a 49–20 roll call vote, but not before the sum authorized was set at $1.75 billion, thirty-six per cent of community action funds were earmarked for the Head Start program, and the adoption of the Byrd amendment, which prohibited payment of salaries to any local antipoverty workers or benefit payments to any participants who belong to subversive organizations or who incite riots.

A conference committee was selected to iron out the differences between the House and Senate versions. On October 18 the Senate accepted the conference report by a voice vote; two days later the House adopted the conference report by a 170–109 roll call vote.

The conference committee action represented a triumph for those who were prepared to impose a number of important restrictions on the structure and administration of the program. Only $332 million was authorized for unspecified community action activities; the bulk of community action money was specifically earmarked for Head Start and for several new congressionally-inspired programs designed to rehabilitate narcotics addicts and provide emergency family loans and special jobs for the hard-core, unemployed poor. The conference also retained the specific requirement that one-third of local community action board members were to be representatives of the poor.

The determination of the House to move in this direction was further confirmed by the action of the House Appropriations Committee which called for a $1.563 billion appropriation and retained the specific restrictions on OEO-administered programs. The House voted in support of the recommendation of its Appropriations Committee. The Senate voted for a $1.663 billion appropriation. A conference committee finally settled for an appropriation of $1.6125 billion.

UNORTHODOXY, RISK, AND MISHAP

Community action as it appeared in the Johnson antipoverty program represented a new and revolutionary technique of social action in which federal funds and federal technical assistance were to be used by local groups of poor people to challenge existing welfare, educational, and political patterns and institutions. The program from the beginning was unorthodox in several respects, each unorthodoxy implying a corresponding risk. A new executive agency, rivaling the Bureau of the Budget as a presidential coordinating arm, was established under a charismatic leader. The risks were that the President would remain committed and alert to the needs of the program, the agency, and the leader, that the leader would remain charismatic, that the internal administration would prove at least adequate to the large task, and that there would be no centrifugal forces at work within the administration of the program.

The mishaps were many. Vietnam drew heavily on the President's time and attention. Community action brought political headaches which may not have been clearly anticipated by the White House. One suspects there was a growing disenchantment with Sargent Shriver which may have been in part a by-product of the strains which developed between the Johnson administration and Senator Robert Kennedy. The image of Shriver as a superlative administrator became tarnished as the new program encountered centrifugal forces, including a few which appear to have been sponsored by the administration.

The mounting of new, immensely varied, and largely untried programs at an unprecedented pace assumed that there would be adequate policy direction at the top and enough good administration in Washington and in the field to make it effective. The program also was launched in a way which seemed to assume a tolerance by Congress of pragmatic, flexible, and experimental approaches. If these assumptions seem to have been unrealistic, it is a fair question whether a more systematic top administrator might have helped. (Would he, though, have had the color and flair so necessary in launching the attack swiftly and with dramatic effect—values highly prized by the Johnson administration?) The assumption that Congress would remain either tolerant or sympathetic for long seems unwarranted in the absence of a congressional majority deeply committed to the antipoverty program with all of its unorthodoxies. The congressional involvement in initiating the program could hardly have been more peripheral. Nor was the congressional role strengthened when, through sheer bad luck, the key House committee became a shambles as its chairman lost control of his own committee.

There was a deeper unorthodoxy, a political one: the involvement of the poor in decision-making. The risk was that the concept would have strong presidential support and that Congress would be willing to tolerate a rather new kind of social experimentation in localities and neighborhoods. The mishap was not a minor one; the support was not there when the chips were down. Even the poor people whom the program was to help proved difficult. They were not content to move slowly nor were they satisfied with minimal or token representation. The technicians in OEO were being taught a painful lesson; once the lid on Pandora's box had been loosened, the poor were not content with its being only partially open.

By the end of 1966, OEO reluctantly began the process of cutting back its community action program. The one domestic program which President Johnson originally wanted most to make his own and which he launched so spectacularly in 1964 found itself two years later in serious difficulty in Congress, among the poor people it was designed to serve and, oddly enough, within the Executive Office of the President. It has frequently been noted that the Office of Economic Opportunity has been engaged in a struggle with at least two departments, Labor and HEW. The ultimate fate of OEO is more likely to be determined by the subtle manner in which the Bureau of the Budget has gradually taken the measure of its Executive Office rival.

CHAPTER 6

HEAD START—AND REVERSE

> "This country thinks it has got full employment. As far as Economics of Employment are concerned, that is probably right. As far as humanities of unemployment are concerned, it is dead wrong."
>
> W. WILLARD WIRTZ (1966).

S HORTLY AFTER THE war on poverty was launched, two pro-grams emerged as definite congressional favorites, the Neighborhood Youth Corps and Project Head Start. Although neither figured prominently in the thinking of the original task force, each got off to a fast start and won ready acceptance in thousands of communities. Head Start was a Sargent Shriver spectacular from the beginning. The Neighborhood Youth Corps has been largely outside Mr. Shriver's control throughout its existence. Based on the work-training concept in Title IB, the Neighborhood Youth Corps is administered by the Department of Labor on authority delegated by Mr. Shriver to the Secretary of Labor. Jack Howard, the Director of NYC, was appointed by Secretary of Labor Wirtz; most of the people administering the program were selected from the career ranks of the Labor Department. Although its funds are derived from the annual appropriation supporting the Economic Opportunity Act, the Neighborhood Youth Corps has never carried the Shriver label as Head Start has.

Project Head Start probably has been more clearly identified with Mr. Shriver than any other OEO activity, including community action and the Job Corps. Mr. Shriver would be expected to resist strenuously any attempt to transfer its administration from his office to the Office of Education in HEW which, incidentally, is precisely what Congressmen Quie and Goodell proposed early in

1966. Head Start got underway with a splash during the summer of 1965, although the planning started earlier that year. Drawing heavily on the experimental studies of Dr. Martin Deutsch of New York Medical College, who worked with small groups of children to develop new techniques for stimulating the intellectual and emotional development of pre-school youngsters from severely disadvantaged backgrounds, Project Head Start was launched as a nationwide program, complete with White House endorsement, almost overnight.[1]

The project was developed within the community action branch of the OEO national office, and community action funds were used to underwrite the first summer of Head Start activity. *Thus, the first major use of OEO community action funds for purposes other than the development of local community-wide action programs was initiated by OEO itself.* Despite the limited nature of community action funds, Congress in 1966 (as noted in Chapter 5) eventually found a good many other uses for CAP monies. In any event, the total cost of the first summer of Head Start activity was $94.5 million, of which OEO provided $85.4 million, the balance coming from local communities. In 2,398 communities across the land, 561,000 children enrolled in the eight-week program.

There was little time for systematic assessment and evaluation that first summer; the emphasis was on getting the project launched in as many communities as possible and on reaching as many children as possible. Nevertheless, the immediate popular impression was that Head Start was an almost universal success. It was, after all, bringing badly needed educational, health, and guidance services to children aged three to five, who, through accident of birth into poor families, would enter the competitive struggle in the world's richest society terribly handicapped even before they reached the first grade of school. Consequently, the Johnson administration's request that $180 million of community action funds in fiscal 1966 be earmarked for Head Start seemed modest enough; this was raised the following year to a request for $310 million which OEO said would make possible not only a substantial summer program but also year-round activities for 210,000 youngsters. If achieved, this would represent a virtual doubling of the enrollment in fiscal 1966.[2]

This chapter traces the evolution of one particular Head Start project which OEO funded during the first summer (1965) and which was administered by the Child Development Group of Mississippi. It is a project which merits close examination because it illustrates most of the fundamental problems involved in fighting the war against poverty.

The first grant of $1.4 million was made in the name of the Mary Holmes Junior College, a Negro school with about 225 students in West Point, Mississippi. The Head Start program, however, was to be operated by the Child Development Group of Mississippi (CDGM). The operating control center was located about two hundred miles from West Point at the Mount Beulah Center near Jackson. The Mount Beulah Center is operated by the Delta Ministry, a civil rights arm of the National Council of Churches. The first director of the CDGM Head Start project was Dr. Tom Levin, a New York psychologist with eighteen years of experience in civil rights campaigns who had worked on the Mississippi Summer Project in 1964. Although Dr. Levin was replaced on orders from OEO after a few weeks, some six thousand children, most of them Negroes, all between the ages of three and five, were finally enrolled in the first summer program. They were taught in eighty-four "centers" in twenty Mississippi counties by a staff which included many veterans of the civil rights movement. One finds it easy to imagine the difficulties which might be encountered in Mississippi in recruiting the dedicated and idealistic individuals who were to teach these six thousand deprived youngsters. Some "centers" were typically small Negro churches; other were renovated abandoned houses; while some classes were held outside in the shade of trees. In at least one case the Head Start meeting place was on the site where a church had been burned *after* being used for classes earlier in the summer.[3]

SENATOR STENNIS INVESTIGATES CDGM

The CGDM Head Start project was scarcely underway when it attracted the attention of the Mississippi congressional delegation led by Senator John Stennis, bedrock segregationist and powerful senior member of the Senate Appropriations Committee. As a result, the first congressional investigation of the Johnson anti-poverty program came from the Senate Appropriations Committee at the insistence of Senator Stennis, and it came in 1965. The Senate Appropriations Subcommittee's investigators reported finding a fair amount of mismanagement in the Mississippi project.

It seemed clear that the CDGM staff was having difficulty meeting ordinary administrative standards, a rather common failing of those local community action groups which make full use of non-professionals. At the same time Mr. Shriver's own investigation found essentially the same problem. Administrative weaknesses are correctable, as has been shown by the experiences of Mobilization for Youth and Haryou, two projects in New York City which had trouble meeting federal administrative standards. What surely concerned Senator Stennis far more than sloppy bookkeeping was the presence among the CDGM staff of people who were active in the civil rights movement in Mississippi.

As a result of the Senate subcommittee's investigation, the Senate Appropriations Committee sponsored an amendment in 1965 which obligated Mr. Shriver to make certain that OEO grant recipients were qualified to administer funds and programs and would make their records available to the General Accounting Office, Congress' favorite fiscal watchdog.

After Senator Stennis presented his criticism of the CDGM Head Start program, Sargent Shriver testified: "Because of this program, 5280 Mississippi children received the education, the medical care, the social welfare services, and in some cases even the clothes, the like of which they never before enjoyed." Mr. Shriver also said that the administrative standards which the Senate had established for OEO were no different from those his agency had been following. "The Senate was aware that we were doing these things already, but it wanted to call our attention to the importance of doing them," he said.[4]

OEO REFUNDS CDGM

It is clear that Mr. Shriver knew at least as early as November, 1965, that the CDGM group in Mississippi would need considerable help from OEO in strengthening their administrative capacity. It was clearer still that Senator Stennis was distinctly unhappy to have a Head Start program operating in Mississippi outside the segregated school establishment. Nevertheless, OEO courageously moved ahead, giving a great deal of attention and technical assistance to CDGM. On February 22, 1966, the Office of Economic Opportunity announced final approval of a $5.6 million grant to CDGM to expand its Head Start program in Mississippi. Presumably the administrative weaknesses were being corrected rapidly, for a grant of this size was to make possible an expanded program reaching some nine thousand youngsters in 175 centers in twenty-eight Mississippi counties.

The very next day, Senator Stennis, speaking on the floor of the Senate, charged OEO with "remarkably poor judgement . . . [and] a complete disregard for the law passed by Congress." The Senator was joined in the attack by his even more segregationist colleague, Senator James O. Eastland, and by Representative John Bell Williams (all three gentlemen are Mississippi Democrats).[5]

And so CDGM expanded its Head Start program in Mississippi. Seven months later, on October 2, OEO announced that it was cutting off funds to CDGM because of serious fiscal and administrative mismanagement practices and program deficiencies, and that a new group would take over the Mississippi Head Start Program. The new group, Mississippi Action for Progress (MAP), was granted two million dollars immediately as part of an eventual ten-million-dollar program. OEO funded the new organization with embarrassing haste, even before the application reached Washington.[6]

If OEO acted with extraordinary speed in funding the new organization, the reaction to the cut-off of CDGM funds was instantaneous. Mr. Reuther's Citizens Crusade Against Poverty charged that the poor people of Mississippi had been "sacrificed to political expediency." CCAP, acting as the conscience of the antipoverty program, immediately established a board of inquiry to make its own evaluation of CDGM's Head Start program in Mississippi. The board, comprised of A. Philip Randolph, elder statesman of the Negro civil rights movement, Dr. Kenneth B. Clark, the distinguished social scientist and renowned student of the Negro ghetto, and Dr. Robert Coles, Harvard psychiatrist, after a quick examination of CDGM activity in Mississippi, concluded that the program was ". . . of the highest order and must be considered a striking success." As a personal aside, Dr. Coles added: "If we are fighting a war against poverty, then this program is actually reaching the poor children and doing so in a way that makes any doctor feel truly impressed."[7]

WHO CREATED MAP?

In the meantime, however, CDGM had been cut off from federal funds and MAP came into being. How it came into being remains a matter of some conjecture. The *Christian Science Monitor* reported: "It is widely known here [in Washington] that the White House played a considerable behind-the-scenes engineering role in setting up M.A.P." An official of MAP told a *New York Times* reporter that the new group was formed at the request of high officials in the Office of Economic Opportunity. The first telephone call, according to this account, came late in August. Following this, five Mississippians—three whites and two Negroes—met with Sargent Shriver and other federal officials in Washington early in September. The form of the new organization was agreed upon at a second meeting held a few days later in Memphis.[8]

At about the same time, Dave Emmons, a young white volunteer handling press relations for CDGM, said that the Mississippi Action for Progress group had been set up in conversations between Harry McPherson, special counsel to President Johnson, and Douglas Wynn, a Greenville attorney with White House connections. Emmons said that Wynn was responsible for asking Hodding Carter III, a liberal and editor of the *Delta Democrat Times* in Greenville, to serve as a board member of MAP. Mr. Carter subsequently denied this, claiming that all contact was made directly by officials of the Office of Economic Opportunity.

Whether it was White House or OEO initiative at work, there can be little doubt—as Walter Reuther's Citizens Crusade review board was quick to point out—that OEO had set about creating a new organization to administer Head Start activities in Mississippi "long before it made its announcement . . . when it was still proclaiming that no final decision on CDGM was reached."[9]

Among the members of the board of MAP were LeRoy Percy of Greenville, and Charles Young of Meridian, both members of LBJ's "President's Club" (whose members contribute $1,000 each), neither carrying conspicuous credentials as representatives of the poor. On the other hand, they were to be joined on the board by Hodding Carter III and Aaron Henry, president of the Mississippi chapter of NAACP. No matter how the new board was constituted, the central question concerning OEO's basic purposes was now clearly open to public view: how far should OEO go in promoting social and political change within a community; how far *could* it go and still obtain a high level of funding from an appropriations committee on which Senator Stennis' influence is far from minor? If OEO has seemed a little reluctant to face courageously all of the implications of a program which uses federal funds to encourage the challenging of local power structures, the conservative bias which is built into congressional appropriations politics may help explain executive ambivalence toward this "controlled revolution," as Nathan Glazer has labeled it.

TROUBLE AT HEADQUARTERS

The reaction within the professional staff of the OEO in Washington to the CDGM fund cut-off was bitter. Some members of the staff were willing to admit privately that the Harlem community action program (Haryou-Act) had been in much worse shape administratively than CDGM; yet the former program was never cancelled, although funds were held up while corrective administrative action was taken. Some OEO officials had a simple explanation for the difference: "Of course, that's Powell's territory."[10]

One thoughtful observer summed up the staff reaction in the following manner:

. . . whatever success MAP may have in the future, it won't easily remove the impression that Mr. Shriver backs away when the political pressures get heavy.

It only lends credence to his critics who charge that once again . . . Mr. Shriver has retreated.

It makes his own staff wonder if every time a program really reaches the poor, begins to stir their motivations, and ultimately involves them meaningfully in the process of protesting against conditions which perpetuate poverty—the man who speaks so eloquently for this kind of involvement will shy away from the ultimate consequences.[11]

So serious had the problem of agency morale become that two of the highest ranking officials in OEO appeared at a meeting of co-workers, an occurrence almost without precedent in the annals of Washington bureaucratic folklore. Bertrand M. Harding, deputy director and second only to Mr. Shriver, and Hyman Bookbinder, assistant director and talented trouble-shooter, appeared before some 150 OEO employees on the evening of October 24, 1966. Mr. Bookbinder said the meeting had been called to put an end to "whisperings in the hall." While the two men conceded that OEO may have been "badly wrong" in the way it handled the CDGM project, they insisted that it was not the result of political pressure from Senators Stennis and Eastland. They were responding to a staff feeling that the front office had pushed the panic button and cut off CDGM funds to insure congressional passage of their appropriations act.

Not so, said Messrs. Harding and Bookbinder. They told the group that CDGM developed problems in 1965 and that OEO, deciding to take a chance on it in 1966, spent more time and money trying to make it work than it had on many other grantees. But, they continued, bad management practices persisted. Finally, it was the judgment of Mr. Shriver and other agency executives that there were "faults that could not be ignored" and they decided "not to refund CDGM at this time when the program was in this condition," Bookbinder said.

Harding added: "Shriver wished he had CIA money, which is not accountable. He doesn't have it and must account for every cent. If he has a grantee who cannot spend that money properly, then he cannot fund it.

"It is up to you to believe whether the decision was made by Shriver on the advice of OEO executives or because of interference by Stennis. There were too many abuses that could not be ignored. It was a heartbreaking decision."[12]

Apparently both the pressure which the Citizens Crusade brought to bear and the floodlight of publicity helped OEO find a way of continuing its support of the CDGM project. On January 30, 1967, after months of negotiation, OEO announced a grant of $4.9 million to CDGM, making possible a program which would serve 5,900 children in fourteen Mississippi counties. Previously CDGM carried on Head Start activities in twenty-eight counties. It had requested a $20 million grant which would have enabled it to serve 13,500 children in thirty-seven counties. In the meantime, of course, MAP had been funded and was administering its own Head Start program in several other Mississippi counties.

WHITHER OEO?

A sense of impending doom permeated the Office of Economic Opportunity as 1966 drew to a close. Deputy director Bertrand Harding was reported ready to transfer several small manpower-related programs to the Labor Department. If administrative logic called for the transfer of these programs to the department most concerned with manpower activities, the same logic might suggest the desirability of moving education-orientated programs to the

Office of Education in HEW. As a matter of fact, such a proposal had been advanced by the Republican members of the House Education and Labor Committee early in the year and not all of their Democratic colleagues were prepared to disagree. Hence, the election of November 8, 1966, which proved to be a disaster in terms of any expansion of Great Society programs threatened to stop OEO as an independent creative force. At least forty-five members of the House of Representatives who had been supporters of the antipoverty program lost their seats in that election. A survey of their successors by *Congressional Quarterly* revealed certain trouble for the Johnson war on poverty. Indeed, had the change in House membership occurred before the most recent amendments to the Economic Opportunity Act were voted upon, the extension of the program would have been in considerable doubt.[13]

What worried people within OEO most was that the centrifugal forces which began picking up speed late in 1966 might soon accelerate and spin off other programs which were administered directly by OEO. This would include two major programs, the Job Corps which would probably go to the Labor Department and Head Start which would move to the Office of Education—in the past a notorious graveyard for bright hopes. Congress had already transferred the small-business loans program to the Small Business Administration, adult basic education to the Office of Education, and Work Experience (Title V in the original bill) was to be administered jointly by HEW and the Labor Department. Thus, OEO, if it survived at all, would be left with only a reduced community action (Title II) program. OEO professionals knew better than anyone else how vulnerable community action would be to congressional critics and to counter pressures from the mayors if it were left in a position of administrative and political isolation. The only eventuality which OEO community action technicians feared more was that Title II responsibilities might be turned over to the new Department of Housing and Urban Development, a possibility which had been recommended to the President (and turned down) early in 1966.

A STRANGE PRESS BRIEFING

The tensions and frustrations within the OEO staff were laid bare at a strange press briefing which had been called, ironically, to advise the press on the proposed transfer of certain functions to the Labor Department. The briefing took place early in November and was best described by William Selover in the November 9, 1966, *Christian Science Monitor:*

> One Shriver deputy, representing the official line, told newsmen that the move to "spin off" some of the work programs, "far from being a giveaway to the Department of Labor, is a strengthening of the Community Action Programs."
>
> "It was clear throughout the legislative history" that manpower programs "to the degree feasible . . . should be administered by the Department of Labor."
>
> But before the briefing could end, the dissension broke into the open.
>
> In a move that took everyone completely by surprise, another top OEO administrator spoke out against the move to "spin off" the programs to Labor.
>
> "We find it difficult to see how we spin this off without spinning off CAP itself," said the official, expressing what appeared to be the substantial sentiment of lower echelon officials in attendance.
>
> The faces of those presiding became mildly ashen.
>
> Reporters, limited by "not for attribution" guidelines, were writing furiously.
>
> This official who has charge of a considerable chunk of the program said he doubted that the legislative history of the two programs in question would support the shift to the Labor Department.
>
> "He was completely out of order saying those things," an official grumbled later.

It was probably inevitable that such a sharp internal split in the Office of Economic Opportunity would not long respect the anonymity of the adversaries, and certainly not if the disagreement were aired at a press briefing. Hence, the press was able to identify Bertrand M. Harding, Mr. Shriver's principal deputy, as being in favor of placing all related youth and adult job opportunity programs under one administrative roof. Likewise, Theodore M. Berry, OEO's community action chief, was identified as the man at the press briefing who expressed serious reservations about the proposed transfer of at least two job creation programs to the Labor Department. It was generally believed that Harding's view would prevail since his opinions were thought to carry weight with the White House while Berry's position had been considered in jeopardy for many months.[14]

Sargent Shriver and Secretary of Labor Wirtz announced on December 14 that the Department of Labor had been assigned direct administrative responsibility for a unified manpower program including the Nelson-Scheurer and Kennedy-Javits programs which were authorized in the 1966 version of the Economic Opportunity Act. Under the Nelson-Scheurer proposal, jobs would be furnished hard-core unskilled unemployed persons in conservation, beautification, health, education, and welfare projects. The Kennedy-Javits amendment called for a special effort which would combine public and private efforts to fight hard-core unemployment in urban areas. Jack Howard, director of the Neighborhood Youth Corps (Title IB of the original act) was appointed administrator of a new Labor Department bureau and authorized to direct all Economic Opportunity Act programs which had been delegated to the department.

A SHORTAGE OF FUNDS

There was another reason for the malaise of despair and disappointment which swept through OEO late in 1966. OEO no longer had the funds to sustain its current level of community action program activity. It had only one alternative: to cut back wherever possible. At a news conference just before Thanksgiving, Sargent Shriver explained that rural areas and communities which started late in developing their Title II projects would be hurt by the reduced level of community action funding. But, he also pointed out: "The impact will be especially harsh on those cities which were able to organize themselves early and which have successful on-going programs."[15]

Mr. Shriver cited the effects on forty-eight cities. New York, for example, which would need $23 million simply to continue existing community action projects would probably get about $16.2 million for the same projects as their share of the national total. Mr. Shriver's comments on the results of the latest congressional action were uncharacteristically caustic: "The poor will feel they have been shortchanged. They will feel they have been double-crossed. The poor will feel that democracy is only for the rich."[16]

What Mr. Shriver did *not* say was that a war on poverty program which had encouraged some 1,100 community action projects around the country to come into being could not possibly be anything more than a cruel hoax when supported by an annual appropriation of a little more than $300 million. Nor was it to be expected that Mr. Shriver would call attention to what appeared to be at least as much a failure of presidential leadership as it was a case of congressional myopia. The truth was that the CDGM episode was merely symptomatic of a much deeper sickness. Carl T. Rowan reported late in October: "The poverty program suffers from a crisis of leadership created almost totally by the White House."[17]

The *Washington Post,* whose editorial page and even its reporting had been generally favorable to OEO and the program, ran a lead editorial on November 4 entitled "OEO in Decline." The *Post* placed responsibility squarely on the President:

> The President can preserve the OEO as a strong independent force only by giving it a large degree of personal protection and leadership. If, in view of the Vietnamese war and other crises, the President concludes that he cannot devote a great deal of attention to OEO, then he can best preserve its achievements by dividing it among the Departments with surgical speed.

If the evidence available to the careful reader of the national press indicated the serious plight of OEO, it is fair to assume that the same evidence, and presumably more, was available to the President. Where had President Johnson gone? The President declared war on poverty in 1964. It was *his* kind of program. The Economic Opportunity Act was *his* bill, much more so than federal aid to education or the tax cut or civil rights legislation or Medicare. Sargent Shriver was *his* chief-of-staff. President Johnson established the priorities.

The conclusion is inescapable: Lyndon Baines Johnson became so involved in a war in Vietnam which he did not start and did not want that he soon lost sight of the war on poverty which he initiated and which only he could lead if it were to be fought with courage and skill. A controversial social welfare program, conceived in the Executive Office of the President and readily ratified by the Congress in 1964, became peculiarly vulnerable to congressional and bureaucratic controls—and to local political resistance—once presidential leadership was deflected.

CHAPTER 7

NEGRO POVERTY
AND NEGRO POLITICS

"America is free to choose whether the Negro shall remain her
liability or become her opportunity."

GUNNAR MYRDAL,
An American Dilemma (1944).

"It is obvious that the urban crisis stems in large part from the
failure to resolve the problems that confront the Negro, and it
is obvious what the Negro wants. He wants what the white Americans are able to take for granted."

WHITNEY M. YOUNG, JR. (March 1, 1967).

NO ASSESSMENT OF the Johnson war on poverty should be
attempted until one understands something about the incidence of poverty in this country, its location, and who its principal
victims are. Who would suffer most if the antipoverty program
initiated by President Johnson were curtailed?

Our kind of poverty is not the poverty of the Asian masses nor
even the poverty of a banana republic. Our poverty, as Michael
Harrington reminded us, seldom lets people starve, although some
of our poor people may go hungry. Our poverty erodes the spirit
while the body, feeding on cheap starches, is as likely as not to be
both fat and anemic. Poverty in the United States, if it means
anything, decrees that its victims shall not participate in the diverse
opportunities which the world's richest economy provides almost

as a matter of course for those millions of its citizens who are not poor. As a social phenomenon, poverty in this country means poor schools, bad neighborhoods, some of the worst housing in Western industrialized civilization, poor health, and extraordinarily poor prospects for effecting any fundamental change in the "system." Not surprisingly, our brand of poverty breeds political apathy and alienation among people on a scale which staggers the imagination.

There are all kinds of poor people in this country: the aged, families on relief, Negroes, Mexican-Americans, Puerto Ricans, Indians, displaced coal miners, migrant farm families, the unskilled, the uneducated, and, always, the young. Those who design public policies to alleviate poverty soon find the diversities within the poverty population so great that no single program approach is sufficient to reach all, or even most, categories. Each group tends to require a different technique, and whatever techniques are employed must somehow be made to "fit" with a rapidly changing economy. Furthermore, no one knows exactly how many poor people there are in the United States because there has been no agreement on a single standard for measuring poverty. Michael Harrington placed the figure between forty and fifty million individuals. The men who planned the Johnson war on poverty came up with a different figure—thirty-three to thirty-five million—but they were using a different standard of measurement. And the official standard of measurement has been refined since 1964.

PATTERNS OF POVERTY

Nevertheless, the patterns of poverty revealed by Harrington and the officials in Washington are remarkably similar. There is no better starting point than Chapter Two of the Economic Report of the President, 1964, in which Walter Heller and his colleagues on the Council of Economic Advisers documented the official case for a war against poverty. Chapter Two reveals that:

1. More than nine million families had total money incomes below $3,000 in 1962.

2. Over eleven million of the poor were children.

3. Seventeen million people—5.4 million families—had money incomes below $2,000 in 1962.

4. More than one million children were being raised in large

families (six or more children) whose incomes were below the $2,000 line.

5. Five million "unrelated individuals" had incomes below $1,500; three million of them were below $1,000.

The Council used an admittedly crude standard: $3,000 cash income for a family and $1,500 for an unrelated individual. What it found below the line represented about one-fifth of the nation. The Report was frank in admitting the crudeness of the measurement:

A case could be made, of course, for setting the overall limit either higher or lower than $3,000, thereby changing the statistical measure of the size of the problem. But the analysis of the sources of poverty, and of the programs needed to cope with it, would remain substantially unchanged.[1]

The 1964 Economic Report also revealed that:

1. Twenty-two per cent of the poor were non-white; nearly half of all non-whites live in poverty.

2. Sixty per cent of the people who are heads of poor families have only grade-school educations.

3. One-third of all poor families are headed by a person sixty-five years of age or older.

4. One-fourth of all poor families are headed by a woman.

Since 1964 other technicians using more refined techniques have produced new figures, but there is no indication that they have significantly altered the profile of poverty in the United States. Miss Mollie Orshansky of the Social Security Administration, for example, developed a new poverty index in 1965 which takes into account differing family size and composition as well as differences between living conditions in urban areas and on farms. The Office of Economic Opportunity has since adopted the poverty level index she devised, pending further research. Miss Orshansky found a minimum of 34.6 million Americans living below the poverty level in 1963. Her standard revealed 7.2 million poverty families and 4.9 million unrelated individuals. But she also found 15 million children in these poor families, 4 million more than the Economic Report of 1964 had indicated.[2]

OUR UNDERDEVELOPED NATION

There were, one can readily see, a number of ways in which the men who designed the new federal program might have chosen to attack poverty. The data assembled by Heller and his staff illustrate how complex the reality of poverty is. The United States has not only developed the world's most sophisticated and productive economy, making possible the highest material standard of living, it also has left considerably more than thirty million of its citizens, fifteen million of them young, effectively cut off from those opportunities which only a rich and free society can offer. Anywhere else in the world, thirty-four or thirty-five million poor people would constitute an underdeveloped nation. If they were hard pressed by an aggressive neighbor, we might even send our armed forces to assist them. The serious point is that "The Other America" of which Harrington has written so movingly does present some of the technical aspects of another underdeveloped nation.

As the United States approaches a population of two hundred million, we tend to lose perspective about the relative size of the other America with its thirty-five million poor. There are more than eighty nations on the State Department's list of underdeveloped nations (not all of whom receive American aid). There were only six underdeveloped nations—on the basis of 1963 data—which had more than thirty-five million people. Of nineteen Latin-American Republics, only Brazil and Mexico were larger than our own "nation" of the poor. In Africa only Nigeria had more people. All the rest of some thirty-five underdeveloped African countries had far fewer. There was no country in the Middle East as large; Egypt with twenty-eight million came closest of the thirteen countries in that area. Our own internal "nation of the poor" has twice as many people as Canada. As a matter of fact, a separate nation of American poor would constitute the fifteenth largest country in the world.[3]

What kind of technical assistance we bring to our own "underdeveloped nation" depends in part on how we view its problems. We could, for example, have a major program directed at the three million poor families headed by someone sixty-five or older. This is not a central objective of the Economic Opportunity Act. We might provide a guaranteed family income for those poor families headed by a woman with children rather than our present Aid to

Dependent Children welfare system. This is not a program objective of the current war on poverty although four and a half million people are involved. Forty per cent of our poor families are farm families, but the Economic Opportunity Act lacks a strong program addressed to the basic needs of the rural poor. Sixty per cent of the heads of poor families have only a grade-school education, yet the provisions of the Economic Opportunity Act are not likely to have other than marginal impact on the educational deficiencies of poor adults.*

Two fundamental points need to be stressed. First, the Economic Opportunity Act does not constitute the entire Johnson war on poverty, although it has been presented to the public as the central instrument; hence, its symbolic significance can scarcely be exaggerated. Second, the Economic Opportunity Act represents the application of funds and techniques which are limited to selected aspects of the nation's "poverty and ignorance" problems.

POVERTY AND NEGRO YOUTH

We come now to the single most important fact about the anti-poverty program which Mr. Shriver has the responsibility for: *it is a set of programs, limited at best, which were designed primarily to have their greatest impact on two groups, the Negro poor and young people, categories which are not mutually exclusive.*

Furthermore, there are sound reasons for concentrating on the Negro and on the young. As Miss Orshansky's studies reveal, fifteen million youngsters are caught in poverty's quicksand. Title I of the Economic Opportunity Act creates the youth programs. First things first. Title I is based on the conception that a large number of young Americans start life in a condition of "inherited poverty," and that unless a way is found of breaking the cycle soon, this unusually large group, many of them non-white, will become the parents of still another—and larger—generation of the poor. The Johnson antipoverty attack assumes that the character of poverty in America has changed, and in changing, the new kind of poverty

*One result of congressional review in 1966 was to transfer adult basic education as provided in the 1964 act from the Office of Economic Opportunity to the Office of Education. Thus far, Congress has provided only limited funds for this program, although it was created by Congress. By early 1967 there was reason to wonder whether the limited efforts then underway in most communities would survive another year of congressional parsimony.

becomes infinitely more deadly for the young. The poverty of the nineteen-sixties, Michael Harrington suggests, ". . . is no longer associated with immigrant groups with high aspirations; it is now identified with those whose social existence makes it more and more difficult to break out into the larger society."[4]

The disadvantages of the poor are worsened by the idiosyncrasies of a public education system which places its most inferior schools in the neighborhoods where poor children are concentrated. This is as true in the hollows of Appalachia as it is in the dark ghettos of Northern urban slums. Even when an occasional superior school, through some miracle, is located in a poor neighborhood, one finds that the children of the poor tend to share with their families a low opinion of the relevance of education which encourages the earliest possible leave-taking from school. The tragic folly of this wastefulness is that it occurs at that moment when educational requirements are increasing at an almost geometric rate.

The Economic Opportunity Act is most meaningful, then, when it comes to grips with the most dangerous social problem of the nineteen-sixties: ". . . an enormous concentration of young people who, if they do not receive immediate help, may well be the source of a kind of hereditary poverty new to American society."[5]

Everything that has been said about the changed nature of poverty needs to be doubled when referring to the plight of Negro citizens. Unemployment among Negroes will serve to illustrate the general point because there is a simple standard of measurement. Every month the Bureau of Labor Statistics in the United States Department of Labor publishes an analysis of the employment situation in the country. The results of the analysis as reported in the press tend to emphasize a single figure—an average overall national *rate* of unemployment. This becomes a kind of thermometer reading which tells us something important about the health of the national economy. For example, when President Kennedy came to the White House in 1961, national unemployment stood close to seven per cent, a catastrophic rate. The thermometer reading indicated serious illness.

The trouble with the overall national rate, however, is that it obscures at least as much as it reveals. One needs to get "inside" the national rate in order to see how specific groups are faring. The experience in recent years suggests one reliable rule of thumb: ordinarily the unemployment rate among non-whites will double the overall national rate. As the Kennedy administration's fiscal and monetary policies and its legislative innovations such as the Area Redevelopment Act of 1961 and the Manpower Development and Training Act of 1962 took effect, the unemployment rate gradually dropped, month by month, until finally it reached 5.5 per cent; and there it stayed from 1962 until late in 1964. When Mr. Johnson came to the White House late in November, 1963, the overall rate was 5.9 per cent. The rule of thumb would suggest a non-white rate of unemployment of about eleven per cent. Actually, the rate of unemployment for non-whites in November, 1963, was 10.7 per cent.

The inability of the Kennedy administration to reduce the overall unemployment rate below 5.5 per cent was undoubtedly a key factor in President Kennedy's decision, communicated to Walter Heller in November, 1963, to proceed in formulating the case for an antipoverty program to be submitted to Congress in 1964. President Kennedy knew that the August March on Washington was a powerful demonstration in behalf of jobs for Negroes at least as much as it was for the right to vote.

WALTER HELLER: AFTER ECONOMIC GROWTH?

The role of Walter Heller and his Council of Economic Advisers in advocating a war on poverty is best understood against the background of the Negro job crisis. The principal objective of the original Heller-Kennedy economic policy of the early nineteen-sixties was stimulation of the economy. After the sluggish performance of the nineteen-fifties, the promotion of economic growth necessarily became the central aim of national policy. In terms of the growth objective, Heller's policy was ultimately successful even beyond the expectations of its advocates, especially after President Johnson drove the massive tax cut through the Congress in 1964. But the Heller policy was also aimed at reducing unemployment, and here the going proved to be significantly more difficult. Originally, Heller and the CEA planned on reaching an "interim goal" of 4 per cent unemployment some time in 1963. The rate actually stood at 5.3 per cent in December, 1963. At that point there had been relatively little improvement in a year and a half.

Elusive as the 4 per cent interim goal seemed to be, its attain-

PINPOINTING POVERTY

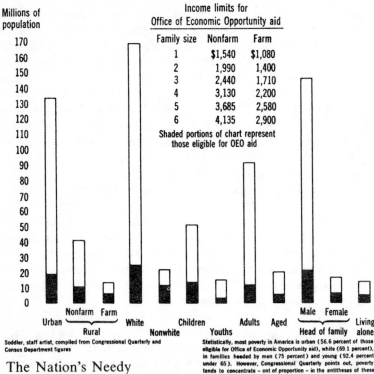

Millions of population	Income limits for Office of Economic Opportunity aid		
	Family size	Nonfarm	Farm
	1	$1,540	$1,080
	2	1,990	1,400
	3	2,440	1,710
	4	3,130	2,200
	5	3,685	2,580
	6	4,135	2,900

Shaded portions of chart represent those eligible for OEO aid

Soddler, staff artist, compiled from Congressional Quarterly and Census Department figures

The Nation's Needy

Statistically, most poverty in America is urban (56.6 percent of those eligible for Office of Economic Opportunity aid), white (69.1 percent), in families headed by men (75 percent) and young (92.4 percent under 65). However, Congressional Quarterly points out, poverty tends to concentrate – ont of proportion – in the antitheses of these groups: rural, nonwhite, in families headed by women and the aged.

ment would leave much to be desired so far as the Negro job crisis was concerned. White America has found it easy to ignore the simple fact that Heller's 4 per cent "interim goal" for unemployment implicitly assumed (albeit not very candidly) an unemployment rate among Negroes of approximately 8 per cent. Walter Heller's advocacy of a war on poverty late in 1963 takes on fuller meaning when one realizes that his original economic policy included the perpetuation of an unemployment condition in the Negro community which can only be termed "catastrophic." To the Negro, a war on poverty was essential because the policy of economic growth by itself offered no prospect of solving the basic problem of chronic unemployment among unskilled Negroes.

The arithmetic of unemployment rates will never be satisfactory until a way is found to clarify the situation in which the young Negro finds himself. A 4 per cent overall rate of unemployment includes an 8 per cent rate for all Negroes. For Negroes between sixteen and twenty-one years of age, the average rate of unemployment during the mid-nineteen-sixties has been close to 25 per cent for males and 33 per cent for females. Our hearts and minds tend to resist the brutal fact that one out of every three or four young Negroes is unable to find a job! In consequence, the reality of despair among young Negroes has never entered deeply into the conscience of white America.*

FULL EMPLOYMENT: FOR WHITES ONLY!

"Full employment" according to the official model of the Council of Economic Advisers contains within it dismally chronic unemployment for Negroes and cataclysmic unemployment for young Negroes. Once this simple, horrible truth is faced, one is better prepared to recognize the fundamental priorities on which the Economic Opportunity Act was based.

The paradox of Negro unemployment becoming malignant in an economy to which economists are willing to attach the label "full employment" is no longer merely theoretical. June, 1966, revealed the nightmarish quality of the New Economics. June, 1966, was a banner month for the American economy, with a record total of 75.7 million Americans at work. The increase by two million in the number of jobs available in June far exceeded any normal expectations for the month. Economic growth, now further stimulated by increased Vietnam war expenditures of perhaps as much as two billion dollars a month, produced more jobs than anyone had a right to expect. June ordinarily tends to be a trying month for those who worry about the job situation as thousands of teen-agers enter the job market seeking both temporary and permanent

*It should be noted that I stress joblessness among Negroes because a decent job is essential to man's dignity. Until we face that basic fact, the ghetto pathology will spread. But I also use unemployment because this is an aspect of the Negro's plight which can, in a sense, be *measured.* I wish to make perfectly clear my position as a social scientist: *measurement* is not my goal. Joblessness among Negroes is simply one aspect of a system of degradation which humiliates, ill-educates, prostitutes, and otherwise horribly violates the human condition of millions of our fellow Americans. For further detail, I strongly urge that middle-class white Americans read the works of James Baldwin and Claude Brown. For those who prefer systematic analysis to autobiography or autobiographical novels, Kenneth Clark's *Dark Ghetto* is social science at its best.

employment. Although all records were broken in June, 1966, as two million teenagers found work, 1,739,000 were *white* boys and girls, while only 270,000 Negro youths were able to find employment. As a result, the unemployment rate among eighteen- and nineteen-year-old Negroes soared to thirty-two per cent, compared with twenty-seven per cent the previous June.

There were other disquieting developments as the economic boom continued. In August, 1966, for example, the Department of Labor reported a rise in total employment but a worsening of joblessness among Negro workers. The 3.4 per cent unemployment rate for whites in August was the same as it had been in April. During the same period, however, the unemployment rate for non-whites gradually increased from 7.0 per cent to 8.2 per cent. In point of fact, by the end of 1966, the unemployment picture in the Negro community represented only a slight improvement over the experience of 1949 and 1950, prior to the Korean war. (See Table 1.)

TABLE 1
AVERAGE ANNUAL UNEMPLOYMENT RATES

	% White	% Non-White
1947	3.3	5.4
1948	3.2	5.2
1949	5.2	8.2
1950	4.6	8.5
1951	2.8	4.8
1952	2.4	4.6
1953	2.3	4.1
1954	4.5	8.9
1955	3.6	7.9
1956	3.3	7.5
1957	3.9	8.0
1958	6.1	12.6
1959	4.9	10.7
1960	5.0	10.2
1961	6.0	12.5
1962	4.9	11.0
1963	5.1	10.9
1964	4.6	9.8
1965	4.1	8.3
1966	3.8	7.3

Put slightly differently, six years of substantial effort under the Kennedy-Johnson administrations succeeded in bringing the Negro unemployment problem to about what it had been in the 1955–57 period prior to the last two Eisenhower era recessions which proved to be so disastrous for the Negro community.

THE GAP WIDENS

There are differences between the mid-nineteen-sixties and the pre-Eisenhower years, and the differences are crucial. The job crisis of the sixties is *far worse* for the young Negro than that faced before Korea. President Johnson recognized this in his memorable address at Howard University, June 4, 1965, when he said: "In 1948 the 8% unemployment rate for Negro teenage boys was actually less than that of whites. By last year it had grown to 23% as against 13% for whites." Nor did the situation improve as the months passed. In 1965 the unemployment rate for non-white boys between the ages of fourteen and nineteen averaged 22.6 per cent. Among non-white girls of the same age, the figure was 29.8 per cent. The year 1966 represented little improvement for this group of young Americans.[6]

An intensive study of ten of the nation's largest urban ghettos conducted by the United States Department of Labor in November, 1966, found that ". . . unemployment—or subemployment—in the city slums is so much worse than it is in the country as a whole that the national measurements of unemployment are utterly irrelevant." The unemployment rate in the slums turned out to be nearly three times the national rate, while one out of every three residents in the slums was found to have a serious employment problem. The causes: ". . . inferior education, police and garnishment records, discrimination, fatherless children, unnecessarily rigid hiring restrictions and hopelessness."[7]

At a time when the economic plight of the masses of poor Negroes shows marked resistance to improvement, even in an expanding and rich economy, the political power of the Negro, both actual and potential, is far from negligible. If the drive of the American Negro to attain his full rights as a citizen now seems to be moving toward full momentum, it may be that the changing pattern of Negro political power has more to do with it than any deep change in the moral climate of white America. In any event, the process of change which is underway will be neither easy nor painless. We have learned that a right that would seem easy to secure, the right to vote, is, in fact, not easily protected. The more complex goal of achieving equal opportunity in education, work, and housing is only now beginning, and the resistances are enormous.

GO NORTH, YOUNG MAN

What elements of strength does the Negro community possess which can be used in the most difficult part of the struggle which now unfolds? *The greatest strength of the Negro community lies in its voting power, in its numbers and their strategic location.*

For several decades, especially since World War II, the Negro has been moving out of the South and into the North. Eighty-seven per cent of all American Negroes lived in the eleven states of the Old Confederacy in 1910. In 1950 the proportion of Southern Negroes was down to sixty per cent; the 1960 census revealed that the figure had been reduced to fifty-six per cent; and it continues to decline. *The 1970 census may very well find more than half of all Negro citizens living north of the Mason-Dixon line.* This ever accelerating movement north (and now west), one of the great population movements in the history of our restless nation, also represents a movement into the cities. Seventy-three per cent of all Negroes were living in cities in 1960, making the Negro the most urbanized of all Americans.

Table 2 illustrates the change in Negro population in selected states between 1950 and 1960. Despite its simplicity, it provides an opportunity for meaningful interpretation.

TABLE 2

NEGRO POPULATION

State	1950	1960
Alabama	979,000	980,000
Arkansas	426,000	388,000
California	462,000	884,000
Connecticut	53,472	107,000
D.C.	280,000	411,000
Florida	603,000	880,000
Georgia	1,062,000	1,122,000
Illinois	645,000	1,000,000

Louisiana	882,000	1,000,000
Massachusetts	73,000	111,000
Michigan	442,000	717,000
Mississippi	986,000	915,000
New Jersey	318,000	514,000
New York	918,000	1,417,000
North Carolina	1,047,000	1,116,000
Ohio	513,000	786,000
Pennsylvania	638,000	852,000
South Carolina	822,000	828,000
Tennessee	530,000	586,000
Texas	977,000	1,187,000
Virginia	734,000	816,000
West Virginia	114,000	89,000
Wisconsin	28,000	74,000

The state with the largest group of Negroes in 1960 was New York. But New York was scarcely unique in terms of concentration of Negro population. By 1960 there were almost as many Negroes in Ohio as there were in Virginia's Old Dominion. California had more Negroes than Arkansas, Florida, South Carolina, Virginia, or Tennessee. Illinois had a Negro population of approximately the same size as Alabama, Georgia, Louisiana, Mississippi, or North Carolina. Pennsylvania ranked just behind California and Illinois as a center of Northern Negro concentration.

Table 3 illustrates the increasing concentration of Negroes in selected large cities.

TABLE 3

NEGROES IN CITIES

	% Negro					Estimated Numerical Increases	
	1940	1950	1960	1965	1970	1965	1970
New York	6	9	14	16	19	1.3M	1.5M
Chicago	8	14	23	27	32	960,000	1.15M
Los Angeles	4	9	14	18	23	500,000	700,000
Philadelphia	13	14	26	29	32	610,000	700,000
Detroit	9	16	29	39	47	650,000	800,000
Cleveland	10	16	29	34	38	277,000	305,000
Washington, D.C.	28	38	54	63	68	506,000	574,000

Whitney Young, executive director of the National Urban League, has estimated that there will be eighteen million Negroes living in our urban centers by 1970 and that before long ten major cities of the United States will be more than fifty per cent Negro. He also reports that Newark, which was thirty-four per cent Negro at the time of the 1960 census, is now over fifty per cent Negro, thus reminding us that we write about a picture which changes even as we write.[8]

The movement north of Negroes and their concentration in the great urban centers of the largest Northern industrial states has the greatest possible political significance. From the end of the Reconstruction period until very recently, the vast majority of Southern Negroes were disfranchised. We tend to think, therefore, of the Negro as lacking political power. Increasingly, and especially since Franklin Roosevelt, the Northern Negro, concentrating in the urban centers, has begun to exert rather considerable leverage in presidential politics which is highly susceptible to balance of power movements by urban minority groups. It is no accident that the American presidency responds far more effectively to the Negro job crisis than does the Congress of the United States.

PRESIDENTIAL POLITICS

There are nine large states, all but one in the North, which together hold the key to modern presidential politics—California, Illinois, Massachusetts, Ohio, Michigan, New Jersey, New York, Pennsylvania, and Texas. In 1960 these nine states had a combined total of 237 electoral votes. They also had a combined total non-white population in excess of seven million. In other words, more than a third of all American Negroes were concentrated in nine key presidential states. Mr. Kennedy carried seven of these states (a total of 180 electoral votes) in 1960, while Mr. Nixon was victorious only in Ohio and California. Mr. Johnson carried all nine in his 1964 landslide victory over a candidate whose views were conspicuously unattractive to the Negro voter.

It is a mistake to assume that the American Negro lacks any real power to change the system which leaves half of his people in conditions of poverty and ignorance. The urban Negro vote concentrated as it is in large cities in the largest states is already an important balancing force in presidential politics, and its po-

SLUM AREA JOBLESSNESS

Oakland
(Bayside) 13.0%

Phoenix
(Salt River Bed area)
13.2%

Los Angeles
(South Los Angeles)
12.0%

Detroit
(Central Woodward area) 10.1%

Cleveland
(Hough and surrounding neighborhood) 15.6%

St. Louis
(North Side) 12.9%

New Orleans
(Several contiguous areas) 10.0%

San Antonio
(East and West Sides) 8.1%

Philadelphia
(North Philadelphia)
11.0%

Boston
(Roxbury area) 6.9%

New York
(Harlem) 8.1%
(East Harlem) 9.0%
(Bedford-Stuyvesant) 6.2%

San Juan
Puerto Rico
(El Fanguito area)
15.8%

Cartographer, based on Labor Department statistics

Some urban slum areas in the United States have an unemployment rate three times the national average of 3.7 percent. The figures are based on a sample of households in each area.

tential for exerting even greater leverage in the future is incalculable. In this sense there is an authentic "black power" which yearns for an indigenous leadership that fully understands the nature of American national politics. Until the advent of the New Deal, the Northern Negro was strongly attached to the Republican party, the party of Abraham Lincoln and the Emancipation Proclamation. Since Franklin Roosevelt there has been a pronounced shift to the Democratic party, and the very fact that there has been a shift serves to increase the leverage of the Northern Negro vote on presidential politics.

The Economic Opportunity Act of 1964, a prime example of presidential legislation, was drafted principally for the poor Negro, although public discussion of the program has seldom been completely candid in acknowledging this fact. (There are, after all, many more poor whites than there are poor Negroes in America.) But the urgent necessity of an all-out attack on the pathology of the dark ghetto dictated the prime objective of the war on poverty. Negro Americans have understood this and consequently have built their expectations to the level encouraged by presidential rhetoric. Negro voters in 1964 overwhelmingly supported the man who put the LBJ brand on the war on poverty.

This is not to suggest that Negro political power is completely effective. Obviously it is not. There is, first, the heavy incidence of political apathy and cynicism which pervades all low-income groups, white and black. There is also the fact of concentration of Negro population in the large cities. The same demographic factor which makes possible great leverage in presidential politics also leaves the Negro conspicuously weak in the congressional arena. The most urbanized American faces a system of congressional baronial power with roots deep in the Republican Midwest and in the rural South. Except on rare occasions such as when a neo-fascist Southern sheriff outrages our most elemental sense of decency, it must be said that the cause of Negro advancement tends to suffer from a lack of broad support in the Congress.

THE OLD ORDER CHANGETH

Nevertheless, the South, which has traditionally led the resistance to Negro advancement and which has also dominated the congressional power structure in our time, faces a rapidly changing political pattern at home as the political power of the Southern Negro grows steadily. In 1947 fewer than 600,000 Southern Negroes were registered to vote. Five years later there were one million; in 1964, two million; and in 1966, two and a half million. It is estimated that three million will be eligible to participate in the 1968 presidential election.

Every one of the eleven states of the Old Confederacy today has a significant bloc of Negro voters. Nearly 250,000 Negroes are registered to vote in George Wallace's Alabama; Arkansas has more than 100,000. Texas has more than 375,000 Negro voters, representing sixty per cent of the adult Negro population of that state. There are 270,000 Negro voters in Georgia. As recently as 1964, Mississippi had a mere 28,500 registered Negro voters; today it has 173,000.

Twelve Negroes sit in the Georgia legislature. There is a Negro sheriff in Macon County, Alabama. For the first time since 1881, a Negro sits in the United States Senate. A survey undertaken shortly after the 1966 election revealed a total of 154 Negro members elected in twenty-seven state legislatures. It was estimated that as recently as 1960 there were only thirty-six Negro legislators in the whole country.[9]

There can be little doubt that Negroes, North and South, have a great deal to learn about the effective use of their newly won political power. Nevertheless, the decisive fact is that the Negro has real and substantial political power in his hands *now*. The truly important question he ought to be pondering is how to use this power, for it is also undeniable that the uneducated, unskilled Negro, with or without the vote, is destined to remain a second-class citizen as long as he remains unskilled and uneducated. At the present, job prospects for young educated Negroes have never been better; for young *untrained* Negroes, job prospects have seldom, if ever, been worse. Unless a means is found soon by which the civil rights revolution may be rapidly transformed into a revolution for equal results—a good education and a decent job—the experience threatens to remain meaningless (or worse) for thousands and thousands of young Americans. It would be remarkable if so desperate a situation did not eventually inspire widespread rebellion among alienated youths.

While it is quite clear where the Negro civil rights revolution has been, no one can say with any certainty where it will move next or who its leaders will be. Negro spokesmen, as different in age, style, and philosophy as A. Philip Randolph, Martin Luther King, and Stokely Carmichael, contend for leadership at a time when many "successful" Negroes seem just a little reluctant to identify with a Negro set of goals. Whatever the merits of the case, most Negroes were shocked to see the most powerful Negro congressional leader stripped of his power. No single action of recent years seemed more likely to discourage an interest among young Negroes in "practical politics." A younger, militant generation speaks increasingly (albeit vaguely) of "black power," scorns white liberals (why do they not integrate the suburbs?) and shows relatively little interest in using the political process to advance Negro goals. Seen in the context of the Vietnam preoccupation, a more conservative Congress, and the possibility of a slow-down in the economy, 1967 offered little promise of significant improvement in the economic lot of poor, young Negroes.

Nevertheless, Negro leaders may yet arise who are "practical" politicians in the sense that they will identify with city, regional, and national programs which have a dominant Negro thrust; they may be "practical," too, in the sense that they will organize their constituency in terms of building support for their program. This would be as different from the anti-discrimination efforts of Martin Luther King and Roy Wilkins as it would be from the inverse discrimination activities of the Carmichaels and McKissicks. The Negro community has a need for prophets but it has a greater need for developing a second generation of more concretely *political* leaders.

So long as time remains, there may be reason to hope that the changing political process will yet prove responsive to the grave issues of Negro poverty. Indeed, if the Negro learns to use his political power, he may force the rest of the nation to make a more durable commitment to a decent society and thus to face the moral issues which underlie all politics. One dares to hope that the Negro, by using political power, will succeed in liberating himself finally and, in doing so, that he will invigorate a national society which badly needs a lift in spirit.

CHAPTER 8

THE WAR THAT
DID NOT ESCALATE

"We assume that the President makes decisions . . . Presidents rarely, if ever make decisions . . . in the sense of writing their conclusions large on a clean slate. They make choices. They select options. They exercise judgements. But the basic decisions, which confine their choices, have all too often been previously made by past events or circumstances, by other nations, by pressures or predecessors or even subordinates. . . ."

THEODORE SORENSON,
lecture at Princeton (March, 1967).

WHEN PRESIDENT JOHNSON declared war on poverty in his 1964 State of the Union message, the nation embarked on a long campaign, the end of which could not be foreseen. Since that time the record of the Johnson administration in encouraging the enactment of a program of domestic reform legislation has rivaled that of the New Deal period. After President Johnson entered the White House, Congress enacted the massive tax cut, the Economic Opportunity Act, federal aid to education, Medicare, the Civil Rights Acts of 1964 and 1965, the Economic Development Act, a considerable expansion and revision of existing health and medical research programs, and a host of related measures. Annual expenditures for health, education, welfare, and labor measures which totaled $7.8 billion in the administrative budget for fiscal year 1965 had been increased to an estimated $14 billion three years later. It is ironic that Mr. Johnson who spent much of his time as Senate majority leader resisting the urging of Senate liberals to push ahead with similar legislative proposals should have emerged in this decade as a strong domestic reform President in the tradition of FDR. Yet there is little doubt that Lyndon Johnson found it both natural and easy as president to sponsor and support a vast, expensive, and expansive program aimed at striking at the roots of poverty and ignorance in affluent America. For the truth is that Lyndon Johnson started his congressional career as a protégé of President Franklin Roosevelt.[1]

TWO DIFFERENT WARS

Despite Lyndon Johnson's personal preference for domestic legislation, by 1967 the contrast between the conduct of the two wars—Vietnam and poverty—was almost complete. The war in Vietnam was escalating steadily; the war against poverty seemed in danger of contracting. In Vietnam the use of conventional and limited methods of warfare had failed to bring victory as apprehension increased that our sense of frustration might trigger the use of extreme methods. In the poverty war, the tendency was to seek more conventional approaches in the belief that unconventional methods had not proven themselves. It was widely assumed that the Johnson administration would continue to seek some basis for a compromise settlement in Vietnam. In the struggle against poverty, the danger seemed all too great that compromise might squeeze much of the vitality from the attack. How are these differences between the two "wars" to be accounted for?

At first the war on poverty came almost *too* easily. The booming American economy made possible a massive tax cut and the declaration of war on poverty in the same year. (Subsequently, under the additional stimulus of enormously increased war expenditures, the continuing boom made it plausible to speak of carrying on an escalating war in Southeast Asia and a substantial program of domestic reform; we easily could have "guns and butter.") It was also possible, at least at first, to enact and to fund major new domestic programs without generating a great deal of public excitement about them and without encountering a great deal of political pressure for or against them. During the first two years of the Great Society, a politics of consensus, guided by a master of group diplomacy, seemed to embrace a program of domestic reform rivaling in scope the New Deal. A theory developed that we had finally reached the point at which reform had become "professionalized." A few talented technicians in government had the esoteric facts and were able to move the antipoverty program from drawing board to point of enactment with, of course, an important assist from this powerful president, but with surprisingly little public clamor—so the theory ran.[2]

"Conflict" and "controversy" were notably absent. Nathan Glazer referred to the community action technique (Title II of the Economic Opportunity Act), which is so vital in the Johnson war on poverty, as perpetrating a "controlled revolution."[3] Glazer seemed only mildly skeptical of the rather curious technique by which some of the technicians hoped to use community action as a means of stimulating the poor to apply pressure on the various local bureaucracies for better services the way middle-class Americans do. Later in this chapter we shall examine more closely how much awareness there was at the White House level that this "controlled revolution" also called for "maximum feasible participation" of the poor and the risk that it might falsely encourage among the desperate people in the dark ghettos expectations which could not be fulfilled easily.

Conservative critics of the Johnson antipoverty program like to dwell upon its "political" nature, and they gleefully note those cases where a strong mayor has used the program's resources to serve his own organizational and political needs. In that sense, the political nature of the program is obvious. But this study seriously questions the political *awareness* of the Johnson administration even with respect to *its own power stakes* in a good many OEO-sponsored activities. The evidence available suggests that the Johnson war on poverty was conceived in a mood of political optimism which bordered on naïveté. Or was it intellectual confusion? Some of the planners of Title II appear to have agreed with those social scientists who hold that "the central fact in a free society is the tremendous contagiousness of conflict."[4]

President Johnson's politics of consensus, on the other hand, aimed at achieving substantial reform without unduly emphasizing the necessity for struggle and conflict; in fact, reform was to come while practicing "economy in government."

"AND NOW, CLASS, WHAT HAVE WE LEARNED SINCE LAST SUMMER?"

From *The Herblock Gallery* (Simon & Schuster, 1968).

THE PROFESSIONALIZATION OF REFORM

Daniel P. Moynihan has pointed to the antipoverty program as
". . . far the best instance of professionalization of reform to appear. In its genesis, its development, and now in its operation,
it is a prototype of the social technique of action that will almost
certainly become more common in the future." And what dis-
tinguishes "professionalized" reform from earlier versions of social
reform? "The initiative came largely from within," Moynihan feels.
"The case for action was based on essentially esoteric information
about the past and probable future course of events."[5]

Yet surely this was not the first time that academic and professional people played an important role in formulating a major
new legislative program. The Social Security Act of 1935 probably
drew more heavily on the knowledge of academic specialists than
did the Economic Opportunity Act of 1964. But this time, as
Moynihan views it, ". . . the main pressure for a massive government assault on poverty developed within the Kennedy-Johnson
Administration, among officials whose responsibilities were to think
about just such matters." Thus, we come to a ". . . type of
decision-making that is suited to the techniques of modern organizations, and which ends up in the hands of persons who make
a profession of it." As a result, decisions are ". . . less and less
political decisions, more and more administrative decisions. They
are decisions that can be reached by consensus rather than by
conflict."[6]

Whether the war on poverty was the creature of presidential
consensus politics or professionalized reform, or a combination of
the two, no great sense of struggle, conflict, or commitment was
communicated to the American public, despite the fact that the
program was designed largely in response to the Negro equal rights
crisis.[7] Moynihan has expressed in writing his concern that the
professionalization of reform seemed to be leading to a new kind
of politics which lacks "moral exhilaration." This may help to
explain the curious absence of public attachment to President Johnson as political leader even when his legislative leadership has been
most effective and even though his program embraces virtually
every important reform proposal of the past two decades. We know
that something is destroying our capacity for moral indignation.
Joseph Lyford, in his brilliant study of urban poverty, fears we

have developed our own version of the "good German."[8] We see and hear, but our moral sense has been anesthetized. We tolerate the virtual destruction of children in the ghettos, ignoring what is going on before our eyes. Most Americans are doing so well in the midst of a seven-year boom, further stimulated by an investment of twenty billion dollars a year in Vietnam, that it requires not only a rare sensitivity but also the patient analysis of hard facts to realize that there really are many Americans who are cut off from the opportunities of our rich national experience. It is a pretty fair assumption that most Americans sincerely believe that anyone who wants to work is at work; after all, we have achieved "full employment." There probably was not one American in ten who knew that nearly a quarter of all Negro youths were jobless as we entered 1967.*

The trouble with the war on poverty, then, is not merely that it came too easily for the President, but, more significantly, that it came too easily for the American public. The year that President Johnson declared unconditional war on poverty most Americans got a tax cut. Consequently, two or three years later when a congressional critic charged "extravagance" in the conduct of the war against poverty, the charge may have seemed plausible enough. The figure 1.5 billion dollars sounds ample to someone who had assumed it wasn't costing the taxpayer and who is not quite sure at what or at whom a war on poverty is aimed. Furthermore, by 1967 there seemed to be no one in the Johnson administration in a position to say frankly that the costs of the antipoverty program for a full year would support the war in Vietnam for perhaps one month. Indeed, by that time the costs of American involvement in that tragic little country had increased so that it was no longer politically feasible for the administration to discuss the economics of the war on poverty candidly, lest the contrast destroy what little support the administration had left among the liberals. In any event, a new Congress, the Ninetieth, took office in January, 1967, prepared to cut "non-essentials" in the war-swollen budget. The war on poverty which had been initiated so easily now became just as easily a prime target for congressional budget-trimmers.

The forces that feed our lack of moral acuteness are undoubtedly

---

*Even among those who recognized the problem of joblessness among Negro youths, there was a great deal of uncertainty about possible remedies.

complex, but part of the problem may be the emphasis on quantification in modern social science, now that social science findings are used in formulating public policy. So long as the New Economics was limited to academic model-building, a definition of "full employment" which postulated a four per cent rate of unemployment was perhaps socially harmless. When a public policy whose goal is full employment comes to accept the four per cent unemployment rate, the social results may prove to be monstrous, especially for the millions of individuals of which the innocuous-sounding "four per cent" is comprised. As we have seen, we achieved the technical goal of "full employment" in 1966 when the rate of unemployment dipped below the four per cent figure. At the same time, the rate among Negro youths was close to twenty-five per cent—precisely at the moment white America thought the nation had finally achieved full employment. Is it any wonder that our moral sense becomes dulled?

BUDGETS AND PRIORITIES

It is important also to understand that the willingness of many in Congress to seize upon the war on poverty as a "non-essential" item in 1967 is the direct result of the manner in which the Johnson administration changed *its* budget priorities between 1965 and 1967. If the Johnson administration faced a crisis in confidence in 1967, it was in part the result of the crisis in priorities which afflicted White House thinking. The President's budget choices—and his rationalizations of those choices—helped to weaken his political position and to encourage his congressional opposition.

In January, 1965, President Johnson sent the Congress an administrative budget for the next fiscal year—1966—in which much was made of the fact that expenditures had been held below a hundred billion dollars. The figure used was $99.7 billion and the precision of the estimate appeared not to exceed the limits of ordinary budget gimmickry. Defense expenditures were to be held to $51.6 billion under the watchful eye—and the infallible computers—of Secretary Robert McNamara. At the same time, expenditures for new and existing education programs were allowed to rise to an estimated $2.7 billion—an increase of more than seventy-five per cent in only one year. Health, labor, and welfare expenditures were to increase to $8.3 billion. The emphasis was on the expansion of Great Society domestic programs while hold-ing the line on defense expenditures. In fact, if one were to go back to 1964, the White House theory was that the war on poverty funds were to come from savings effected by Secretary McNamara in his far-flung activities.

The steady escalation of the war in Vietnam has tended to blunt the budgetary optimism which pervaded official Washington throughout 1965. The remarkable performance of the American economy following the massive tax reduction in 1964 brought a level of economic growth which exceeded the expectations of the Council of Economic Advisers. Edwin Dale, Jr. of the *New York Times,* who often popularizes the current mood of the Council, wrote lyrically in November, 1965, about "Uncle Sam's $50 Billion Surplus." "It is now certain," he said, "that if we avoid a major depression the G.N.P. in 1970 will be more than $850 billion, meaning we will have more than half as much growth in the next five years as in the 300 years up to 1950." The resulting growth, Dale continued, would give the American president an additional seven to ten billion in revenues each year to spend on whatever domestic programs he might choose. The real problem was to make certain that the additional $50 billion in revenues between 1966 and 1970 *were actually spent* in order to avoid "fiscal drag."[9] What a delightful prospect for any American president!

Actually, expenditures for defense in 1966 ran considerably ahead of the January, 1965, budget estimates; the final figure was $54.2 billion rather than $51.6 billion. At the same time, total expenditures in the administrative budget showed little respect for the magic $100 billion barrier as they soared to a figure some-what in excess of $106 billion. White House sources were putting out background stories late in November, 1965, pointing to the war in Vietnam as the principal cause of the unexpected increase in expenditures.[10] (This was later to become an end-of-year ritual for the Johnson administration.)

It was therefore at least a mild surprise when President John-son's 1966 State of the Union message revealed a projected deficit in the administrative budget in the coming fiscal year—1967—of only $1.8 billion, the lowest figure in seven years. It was as if a magician had been at work on the figures rather than the seasoned technicians of the Bureau of the Budget. Defense expenditures alone were estimated to increase to $58.3 billion while total expenditures were estimated at a record-breaking $112.8 billion. The continuation of Great Society domestic programs and an expanding war in Vietnam were to go hand in hand with the smallest deficit in years. The booming economy would take care of that.

The reality of fiscal year 1967 suggests that federal budget-making does not fare well in the hands of magicians. In December, 1966, the public learned for the first time that the war in Vietnam was costing almost twice as much as had been estimated a year earlier—$20 billion rather than $10 billion, a margin of error which suggests the Pentagon might consider investing in later model computers. With defense spending rising to $67 billion, the deficit would approach $10 billion rather than the remarkably optimistic January estimate of $1.8 billion. Expenditures in the administrative budget were expected to exceed $126 billion, a far cry from January's $112.8 billion estimate.

A budget so far out of control has serious implications, especially for those who are responsible for economic advice to the administration. Edwin Dale reported that the $10 billion error caused distress, even anger, among government economists (presumably the Council of Economic Advisers) who felt they had been misled by the Pentagon. Their view was that the whole performance discredited the idea of modern, sophisticated management of the economy. Others may have felt that it discredited the ability of the administration to add. Nonetheless, Secretary of Defense McNamara continued his extraordinary record of having made no mistakes in office by simply denying that an error had been made! His position was that the entire $10 billion "discrepancy" could be accounted for by a change in the assumptions on which the budget was based—which seemed a lot to ask even of a "budget assumption."

The McNamara position was summarized by Edwin Dale:

> The starting assumption was that the war would end on June 30, 1967. When it became clear that such an outcome would not materialize, manpower and procurement had to be increased above the targets set in the original budget, each accounting for about half the $10 billion increase. Mr. McNamara points out correctly that the Congress was warned of this possibility, though not with any dollar amounts, as early as last February.[11]

As January, 1967, approached, and with it the necessity for

submitting still another budget (fiscal 1968), the Johnson administration changed its assumptions. It no longer assumed, even for
budgetary purposes, that the war in Vietnam would soon be over
or that it could be funded on a limited basis. It was obvious that
the so-called "small" war in Vietnam was now larger than our
previous "small" war in Korea with annual costs exceeding $20
billion. It seems fair to assume, therefore, that the Johnson
administration budget proposals for fiscal 1968 represented reasonably accurate projections and that its presentation was reasonably candid in revealing the priorities on which the new budget
was based.

The budget for 1968 (we continue to deal with what is known
technically as the administrative budget) called now for defense expenditures of $75.5 billion, representing a $23.9 billion increase
in two years. Total expenditures would rise to a projected $135
billion. There was room in this, the President felt, for modest
increases in Great Society programs. In the specific case of the
Economic Opportunity Act programs, the President asked for $2
billion in contrast to the $1.6 billion which the previous (and
friendlier) Congress had provided for fiscal 1967. Even this modest
increase had doubtful validity, since a considerably more conservative Congress surely would want to trim a $135 billion budget,
especially the "non-essential" items. And there was little doubt
that the war on poverty had become a non-essential. Senator Rus-
sell Long, Democrat of Louisiana, chairman of the Senate Finance
Committee, and Representative George Mahon, Democrat of
Texas, chairman of the House Appropriations Committee—neither
of whom is politically unfriendly to President Johnson—said as
much on the eve of the opening of the first session of the Ninetieth Congress.

POLITICS OF APPROPRIATIONS

Nowhere was the change in the balance of political forces more
clearly demonstrated than in the composition of the key House
Appropriations Subcommittee which is responsible for antipoverty
funds. On the first day of the first session of the Ninetieth Congress, Democratic Representative John Fogarty of Rhode Island,
widely respected chairman of the subcommittee, died suddenly of
a heart attack. Fogarty, whose detailed knowledge of HEW and the

Labor Department as well as the Office of Economic Opportunity was legendary, generally supported an expansion of health, education, and welfare programs. The loss of Fogarty strengthened the influence of Representative Melvin Laird, Republican of Wisconsin, the ranking minority member who rivaled Fogarty in ability, familiarity with the programs, and influence with other powerful men in Congress. Laird was not only considered more conservative than Fogarty, but was to be joined on the subcommittee by several new men, most of whom were not likely to view Great Society innovations with great enthusiasm. Four Democrats who served under Fogarty were defeated in the 1966 election; three of them were staunch liberals. The only remaining Democrat from the "old" Fogarty subcommittee, Representative Daniel Flood of Pennsylvania, succeeded to the chairmanship on the basis of seniority. Flood had a record of supporting Johnson administration domestic programs, but he was destined to preside over a subcommittee which was now leaning definitely to the conservative side. Spending levels recommended by appropriations subcommittees can be overturned by full committee or by the House. In practice, however, the general spending pattern is usually fixed by the subcommittees, and the power of the appropriations subcommittee in overseeing the administration of programs is far greater than most observers realize.[12]

Thus, the war on poverty which went into operation in November, 1964, and which encountered growing resistance in Congress throughout 1966 was now confronted with a bipartisan coalition of views ranging from skepticism to hostility and a mood that favored economy in what was deemed "non-essential." President Johnson, who originally declared unconditional war on poverty in his 1964 State of the Union message, and who shortly thereafter brought forth the Economic Opportunity Act (written in his Executive Office) as his own principal domestic innovation, now faced the unattractive choice in 1967 of either re-enforcing his personal commitment at a time when his political strength was waning or of watching Congress slowly squeeze the vitality out of his program. But to acquiesce in the congressional squeeze was to risk further intensification of the social chaos which already permeated the nation's dark ghettos. None of this seemed likely to improve the President's image in the large Northern metropolitan areas where presidential elections tend to be decided.

It is curious that a president who was regarded by friend and foe as a political entrepreneur of extraordinary acumen seemed willing at times to stake his claim on history largely on his success in effecting a far-reaching program of domestic reform—an area in which his credentials originally were somewhat suspect. Yet sometimes he seemed not to be greatly concerned to protect that claim. Evans and Novak in their penetrating appraisal of Mr. Johnson as a man of power have suggested that in launching the antipoverty program, the President seemed willing ". . . to mortgage the future by planting hopes and expectations among the poor of such magnitude that they could not be met."[13] The legislative package which became the Economic Opportunity Act was not only put together much too quickly to have much coherence, it also appears to have been conceived with an oddly casual attitude toward some of its basic political implications. "Maximum feasible participation" of the poor was the creature of technicians in an administration which is often thought to be compulsively "political." Throughout this study one gets glimpses of the White House which raise doubts that the President had a clear view of what his war on poverty contained or of how far he ought to take it.

MEASURES SHORT OF WAR

Most of the programs created by the Economic Opportunity Act, with the possible exception of the Neighborhood Youth Corps and Project Head Start, have never been budgeted at anything more than a pilot-project level of social experimentation, although both the President and Mr. Shriver have persisted in speaking of the act and its programs in terms of a major, all-out attack on poverty. Widespread disillusionment is the predictable result whenever program activity falls glaringly short of the expectations which the administration's expansive rhetoric has encouraged. The Job Corps, for example, may finally reach an enrollment approaching forty thousand youths in 1967, but Job Corps recruits are drawn from a universe of disadvantaged young people numbering in the hundreds of thousands. OEO proudly reports that it has 1,100 community action programs across the country at a time when its annual budget has not much more than $300 million of "free" funds available for such projects. The ten largest cities alone could absorb that much without seriously denting their poverty-related problems. The technicians in the localities who are trying to put projects together are the first to recognize that OEO simply has not had funds to move most communities beyond the pilot-project stage.

This is one of the difficulties encountered in combining a "war on poverty" with "economy in government." The other is that people tend to overlook the innovations which *are* being made. The whole effort in 1964 and 1965 aimed at holding the budget below $100 billion was designed to make the Johnson program less unpalatable to certain powerful congressional chairmen. But others may fail to see that there *is* a new program. It was not for nothing that Douglass Cater, presidential assistant, found it necessary to abandon temporarily the "passion for anonymity" which his White House staff position presumably imposed in order to write a popular article defending—even describing—the vast program of social reform and innovation which President Johnson had sponsored and much of which had been written into law.[14] One does not recall that Franklin Roosevelt needed White House authors to convince the American public that a New Deal had, in fact, taken place.

In all fairness, it should be noted that the domestic programs sponsored by the Johnson administration continued to expand during 1966, despite the escalation of the war in Vietnam. But the President received far less public credit than he deserved, principally because many Americans seemed quite unaware of the great changes taking place.

Perhaps the most mystifying aspect of the Johnson administration's handling of the war on poverty is the way in which OEO militants were allowed to push ahead their version of community action, making a public showdown with powerful mayors inevitable. Even if the White House were prepared to do battle with big-city mayors, it does not necessarily follow that a national administration would wish to enter the fray in a spirit of abrasive militancy. It is difficult to imagine why so little thought was apparently given at the White House level to the various kinds of political and social upheaval which community action obviously carried with it. Why did the White House pay so little attention to the practical implications of a new social action technique which it was prepared to sponsor *as its own?*

COMMUNITY ACTION AND
PRESIDENTIAL POLITICS

Is it conceivable that the White House did not fully understand the political implications of community action as it was being developed within the Office of Economic Opportunity? (OEO is located in the Executive Office of the President and the director is appointed by the President, so the question is not put lightly.) Did the White House approve and endorse that version of community action which encouraged the use of federal funds in local communities as a means of arousing ghetto residents to apply pressure on city hall in order to effect basic changes in the conditions of life in the slums? Was it not reasonably clear that community action promised, at a minimum, to upset a number of powerful mayors and, at a maximum, to alter profoundly the nature of urban politics? Was the President clear that "maximum feasible participation" of the poor would immediately engage his administration in a bitter struggle with city hall, the welfare establishment, and the educationalists? In short, was the President advised as to what OEO proposed doing under Title II of the Act?

It may be that no definitive answers to these questions can be established at this time, but a number of helpful insights have been presented by Daniel P. Moynihan.[15] Moynihan feels that the problems which were to plague community action were already implicit at the time the proposal was submitted to Congress since there were at least four distinct—and incompatible—understandings of what "community action" intended.

The Bureau of the Budget concept looked to community action as a new method of bringing about better administrative coordination of several overlapping programs. The Alinsky concept stressed the need of the poor to acquire a sense of power by building organizations of their own; this could best be achieved by engaging in conflict—"to rub raw the sores of discontent," in the words of Saul Alinsky. This view found support, as Moynihan confirms, among the staff of the President's Committee on Juvenile Delinquency, which, together with the Ford Foundation, had been sponsoring such projects (Mobilization for Youth on the East Side of New York City was one example) in various cities for some time prior to the Johnson war on poverty. The peace corps concept seems self-explanatory. It involves sending well-motivated and idealistic people to work among our own "underdeveloped peoples." Finally there was the task force concept which merits further examination.

The Shriver task force view of community action has a direct bearing on the issue of the President's involvement in, and his understanding of, Title II of the Economic Opportunity Act. Mr. Moynihan is the only member of the Shriver task force who has written about their view of the process, and he has said quite frankly that the task force was not chiefly concerned with the issues of "efficiency" or "conflict and power" or "youthful idealism." Hence, there was a fourth view—their own—whose guiding principle was political effectiveness. "The Task Force wanted a program that would pass the Congress, help win the Presidential election, and eliminate poverty, in perhaps that order," is the way Moynihan has put it.[16] However, he has also declared that ". . . the program began with this potential—this certainty—that it would often be interpreted in different and incompatible ways. *It was never clear that the persons to be in charge of the program perceived these differences, and no hint of them emerged in the Congressional hearings on the bill.*"[17]

The Economic Opportunity Act was written by the professionals (I would prefer calling them "technicians") and has been described elsewhere by Mr. Moynihan as the best example yet of "the professionalization of reform." Certainly, the evidence in this study points to Title II as the creation of the professionals (technicians). One wonders whether the professionals do not have an obligation to warn their political leaders (the president of the United States, in this case) when the proposal contains incompatible concepts. At least one view strongly held by part of the bureaucracy (first the President's Committee on Juvenile Delinquency and later the community action staff within OEO) actually is loaded with political dynamite. If it is correct that the people in charge of the program never perceived the different concepts, the criticism is grave, because the people in charge were Sargent Shriver and—ultimately—the President. Were the men on top alerted to the potential (Moynihan adds, "the certainty") contained in Title II?

Ordinarily it might be possible to absolve the professionals who wrote the legislative package of this responsibility on the grounds that politics is not their business. In this case, however, we are advised that the task force view of its own role included "political effectiveness" as its principal concern.

ADVISING THE PRESIDENT

Moynihan suggests that the liberal Democrats on the House Education and Labor Committee later were difficult because they had not been alerted to the problems contained within Title II. "These are men," he has written,

> willing to take a good deal of heat for a decent social objective: but they expect to be warned about it in advance, so that they can make up their own minds what risks they will take, and not have the issue settled for them by an anonymous enthusiast rubbing other people's sores. . . .[18]

Fair enough. Is there any reason to suppose that President Johnson, an experienced, seasoned, and resilient politician, would not also be prepared to take a good deal of heat in order to advance a decent social objective? It is conceivable, of course, that the White House was fully cognizant of all that was implied in Title II, including "maximum feasible participation" of the poor and yet, that it willingly undertook the political risks involved. If so, however, the administrative history of OEO's first two years makes relatively little sense. How is the CDGM episode to be accounted for? Was Sargent Shriver in conflict with the White House when he funded it or when he refused to fund it? Or when he finally funded it on a compromise basis? One is not convinced that the White House saw or understood the political "reality" of community action as it was developed by OEO until the program was in operation and had become controversial. And then the administration began to back away, slowly, almost imperceptibly at first.

This may have been easier than one might imagine, since the evidence suggests that the White House originally failed to keep a close control on the development and administration of the antipoverty program. A public airing on the front page of the *New York Times* of basic differences between two White House agencies, the Bureau of the Budget and OEO, over the administrative interpretation of "maximum feasible participation" would be remarkable under any circumstances. Interest and curiosity are heightened when it occurs in an administration which is known to abhor any public display of policy differences, even at the Cabinet level. And in this instance, the fundamental issue remained unresolved—and became public—a full year after the program got underway. The question arises: does this reflect the kind of attention normally paid by a president to a major program with which he has indelibly identified himself? Abnormal though it may have been, President Johnson's lack of interest in the administrative reality of his new program seems to have been there from the very beginning. Evans and Novak, in reviewing the early struggles between Shriver and the departmental spokesmen, report that other government officials soon discovered ". . . how little interested Johnson really was in [those] differences."

Through all these bureaucratic struggles the President seemed largely disinterested and dispassionate. Nor was he to take much of a personal hand in differences between Shriver and the established bureaucracy. He was, in other words, considerably less interested in the content of the program than in his determination to achieve a great national consensus to eradicate poverty. To Johnson, the means were less important than the end.[19]

THE JOHNSON ADMINISTRATION AND THE NEGRO CRISIS

The Economic Opportunity Act of 1964 represents a sizable part of the Johnson administration's answer to the revolution of rising expectations in the Negro community, especially as the Negro revolution reaches beyond mere voting rights. In signing the act in August, 1964, the President said: "Today for the first time in all the history of the human race, a great nation is able and willing to make a commitment to eradicate poverty among its people." Although the President spoke to all Americans, one can be sure that his words of commitment carried a special meaning in the Negro slums, North and South. Less than a year later, speaking at Howard University on June 4, 1965, the President went even further in pledging his support to what he specifically referred to as "the revolution of the Negro American."

A few excerpts from the address will indicate its remarkable nature:

> The task is to give 20 million Negroes the same chance as every other American to learn and grow—to work and share in society—to develop their abilities—physical, mental, and spiritual —and to pursue their individual happiness.
>
> To this end equal opportunity is essential, but not enough. . . .

For Negro poverty is not white poverty. Many of its causes and many of its cures are the same. But there are differences—deep, corrosive, obstinate differences—radiating painful roots in the community, the family and the nature of the individual. These differences are not racial differences. They are solely and simply the consequences of ancient brutality, past injustice and present prejudice. . . .

But they must be faced, and dealt with, and overcome if we are to reach the time when the only difference between Negroes and whites is the color of their skin.

Credibility-gap critics could scarcely find fault with the Howard address which candidly recognized that too many Negroes were losing ground in the battle for true equality. The President cited hard and bitter facts:

Thirty five years ago, the rate of unemployment for Negroes and whites was about the same. Today the Negro rate is twice as high.

In 1948, the 8% unemployment rate for Negro teenage boys was actually less than that of whites. By last year it had grown to 23%, as against 13% for whites. . . .

Only a minority—less than half—of all Negro children reach the age of 18 having lived all their lives with both parents. At this moment, today, little less than two thirds are living with both parents. Probably a majority of all Negro children receive federally aided public assistance during their childhood.

There could be only one reaction among those Washington influentials, of whom Professor Neustadt has written, who watch for signs of presidential policy leadership. Lee Rainwater and William L. Yancey have made an intensive study of the tangled web of circumstances which followed the Howard University address. They conclude that the address seemed to signal an important shift in the stance of the federal government toward civil rights issues.

The "next and more profound stage" of the civil rights struggle would go beyond legal protection of rights, to providing the resources for Negro Americans to turn freedom into an equal life. The emphasis was on the social and economic factors of jobs, housing, education, community and family life.[20]

Yet months and months passed without any new major attack on the pathology of the Negro ghetto. The President's Howard address was followed in the summer by the Watts rebellion and in the autumn of 1965 by a raging controversy over the so-called Moynihan report on the Negro family—a report which provided much of the data for the President's address at Howard. The administration first used the report on the Negro family apparently to suggest a new policy initiative, withheld the report from public distribution for several months, partially misrepresented its contents in the aftermath of Watts, and finally, in effect, rejected the report as a basis for action.[21] By that time, it was hard to find a Negro leader who would say a good word for the report, which, incidentally, had been written originally as an internal document. Printed as a public document and selling for forty-five cents, the report eventually sold thousands and thousands of copies.

CRISIS IN LEADERSHIP

The failure of the Johnson administration to act on the Howard University speech might be ascribed simply to a weakness of executive will if it were not for the curious behavior of most Negro and civil rights leaders in the weeks and months immediately following the momentous address. Responsible Negro leaders seemed unable to move from protest to politics at a moment when many options appeared open. Rainwater and Yancey, on the basis of their extensive investigation, report that the White House staff apparently lost touch with key civil rights leaders during the critical period following the Howard address. Important Negro leaders who had often been consulted by the White House in the past now learned "second-hand" about a controversial Moynihan report on the Negro family through garbled newspaper accounts.

Moynihan, who soon found himself in the center of an almost obscene controversy, has since written of an opposition which came not from the Right but from

> . . . Negro leaders unable to comprehend their opportunity; from civil rights militants, Negro and white, caught up in a frenzy of arrogance and nihilism; and from white liberals unwilling to expend a jot of prestige to do a difficult but dangerous job that had to be done, and could have been done. But was not.

What were the forces outside government to move toward? The Johnson administration, having taken the initiative and having boldly urged a new approach to the issue of Negro equality, now lacked a program of action. Once again the Johnson administration's rhetoric outpaced its willingness to face political and administrative realities. And, once again, the increasing preoccupation with Vietnam blocked White House vision of the domestic scene. It is interesting to note that Moynihan, who helped prepare the Howard address, believes that the White House did not backtrack on the commitment to the cause of Negro equality, although official preoccupation with Southeast Asia "did mean that the White House was not going to think up a program" to support its commitment to American Negroes. "If a program was to be forthcoming," Moynihan has suggested, "it would have to be the work of the civil rights movement, with whatever assistance it could muster in government departments and universities."

Whatever happened to the professionalization of reform? Is it sensible for a president to launch a major policy initiative, as in the Howard address, making a firm commitment to advance the cause of Negro equality and moving the struggle to a new plane, without having a program in mind? Apparently, neither the White House nor civil rights leaders were prepared to advance a program at a moment of decisive importance. But how are we to account for the absence of those professionals and technicians, of whom Moynihan wrote earlier, whose job presumably is to devise such programs for the President? Moynihan may have touched upon a point of surpassing importance when he noted: "The energies of that tiny group at the apex of government were now directed elsewhere."[22]

Whether one accepts Moynihan's view that the Howard address and the immediate aftermath represented a lost opportunity to make a total commitment to the cause of Negro equality, there can be no doubt that two years later American Negroes were still waiting for the all-out attack on the problems highlighted by the President's address. The malignancy was still there, eating away at the vitals. Unemployment among Negroes remained at least twice as severe as unemployment among whites, and there were some initial signs that it might actually be worsening. (If the economy were to slow down even a little, Negro unemployment

THE NEW HOUSE—OPPOSITION
TO KEY JOHNSON PROGRAM GROWS

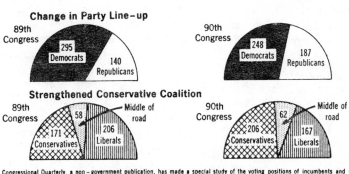

Change in Party Line-up

89th Congress
295 Democrats
140 Republicans

90th Congress
248 Democrats
187 Republicans

Strengthened Conservative Coalition

89th Congress
171 Conservatives
58
206 Liberals
Middle of road

90th Congress
206 Conservatives
62
167 Liberals
Middle of road

Congressional Quarterly, a non-government publication, has made a special study of the voting positions of incumbents and new members of the 90th Congess and compared them with the patterns of the 89th. In the Senate, where the Republicans gained only three seats, change was minimal. But in the House, where the G.O.P. gained 47 (top chart) the study found that the conservative coalition gained appreciably (chart above). This coalition is a traditional grouping of Republicans and Southern Democrats who generally resist expansion of social welfare programs. The effect of this shift on some of Johnson's major programs, as analyzed by Congressional Quarterly, is shown below.

FAVOR ▓▓▓▓▓☐   OPPOSE ▒▒▒▒☐
Democrats Republicans   Democrats Republicans

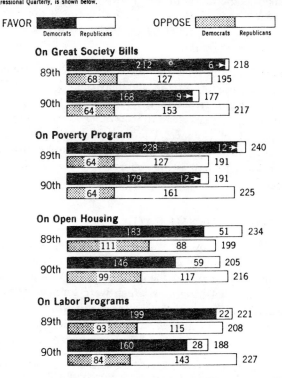

On Great Society Bills

89th
212 · 6→ 218
68 127 195

90th
168 9→ 177
64 153 217

On Poverty Program

89th
228 12→ 240
64 127 191

90th
179 12→ 191
64 161 225

On Open Housing

89th
183 51 234
111 88 199

90th
146 59 205
99 117 216

On Labor Programs

89th
199 22 221
93 115 208

90th
160 28 188
84 143 227

would be expected to rise sharply.) Joblessness—and hopelessness—continued to afflict more than twenty per cent of young Negro males and about a third of all young Negro females. In the meantime, Vietnam absorbed all of the increase in federal revenues—and more—which the sixth year of continuous economic expansion produced.*

The President's attention was directed more and more to the morass of Southeast Asian military and political involvement. His political strength at home had diminished markedly while the balance of power in the Congress had swung back to the conservative bipartisan coalition which had dominated the Congress most of the time between the end of World War II and Mr. Johnson's advent to the presidency.

The prospects for facing up to the problems of the Negro ghetto became bleaker as the mood in the ghettos grew increasingly grim and ominous. Whitney Young, executive director of the National Urban League, not an alarmist by nature, warned a Senate subcommittee in December, 1966:

> Any further failure to meet the needs of the Negro population, any further broadening of the gap between white and Negro citizens in their experience of the possibilities held out by the American dream can only lead to increasing unrest, disorder and a mounting risk of violence. The time is clearly past for half-way measures, token gestures, pilot programs, and half-hearted, one-dimensional, small scale efforts, no matter how well intentioned.[23]

SCRATCHING THE SURFACE

The Johnson war on poverty was only beginning to scratch the surface of ghetto pathology as the antipoverty program entered its third year. In the first place, the Economic Opportunity Act established a number of programs which were limited instruments at best. Secondly, the administrative apparatus which was created to put the new programs into effect left a great deal to be desired. The Office of Economic Opportunity represented an interesting

---

*It has not been possible in this brief case study, focusing as it does on policy and politics, to portray adequately the despair and misery of the Negro ghetto. This study emphasizes one basic aspect, the lack of meaningful opportunities for decent jobs. The reader is, therefore, urged to read Kenneth Clark's great book, *Dark Ghetto.*

and unusual attempt to create a mechanism in the Executive Office of the President—above and apart from the Cabinet departments— which could launch a major program in a hurry, and this it managed to do. But OEO was also created as an agency which would coordinate the related activities of existing departments, and here it has failed, for whatever reasons.[24] At the same time, OEO insisted on operating its own large programs such as community action, the Job Corps, and Project Head Start, with results which were exceedingly mixed.

The administrative difficulties of the Office of Economic Opportunity deserve full and careful analysis; such an analysis lies outside the confines of this book which has focused its attention on the politics of poverty. This study views Sargent Shriver as a man with rare gifts as an inspirational leader. He scores high in public relations and as a Capitol Hill spokesman—qualities which were important in getting a complicated billion-dollar program launched quickly. Yet Shriver has experienced unaccountable difficulty in holding together a team of high-level administrators. Three men— Jack Conway, Bernard Boutin, and Bertrand Harding—have been his principal deputies within a two-year period; the Job Corps had no less than three directors between 1964 and 1966.

Serious errors in judgment at Mr. Shriver's level of decision-making have also plagued OEO from the start. It was a fundamental mistake for a White House-level agency to undertake the administrative responsibility for so many new operating programs. (Ideally, a White House agency which has responsibility for program coordination ought not to operate *any* programs; but the need for innovation was real and there was skepticism about the ability of the departments to innovate.) Community action alone would have been more than enough for OEO, but Shriver personally was determined to make the Job Corps his shining new program. It was also a mistake to encourage the development of hundreds upon hundreds of local community action agencies when the funds and the technical expertise available were so limited that they would only have supported a meaningful initial effort in ten or twelve of the largest cities. Shriver wanted to introduce community action everywhere and anywhere when concentration upon a dozen cities might have led to the discovery of a cure for the ghetto malignancy. The tragic result: the new program ends up fighting cancer with aspirin tablets.

THE FUTURE

What of the future of President Johnson's war on poverty? Obviously, much will depend on the future of the war in Vietnam. The $20 billion-plus annual expenditure in Vietnam has shown us what the level of spending in the public sector might be if there were no war in Asia. But even if the war drags on, Congress may be expected to find funds to support favorite activities such as the Neighborhood Youth Corps and Project Head Start. If the Job Corps survives an almost certain legislative overhaul in the Ninetieth Congress, it is likely to find an administrative home outside the Office of Economic Opportunity. If the Office of Economic Opportunity survives, its role and responsibilities may be changed substantially. Some of the antipoverty program's best friends in Congress seem to have reservations about OEO as an operating agency of government. The liberal Democratic members of the House Education and Labor Committee are among those who see a more limited role for OEO, and their Republican colleagues are not likely to disagree. Senator Abraham Ribicoff, Democrat of Connecticut, after chairing an investigation of the crisis in the cities, recommended that OEO concentrate its efforts on coordinating the bewildering array of federal programs which bear upon the issues of poverty and ignorance. Senator Ribicoff would transfer operating programs to the departments, leaving OEO to serve as catalytic agent for new experimental and demonstration programs. Senator Joseph Clark, who serves as chairman of a Senate subcommittee on manpower, planned to devote most of 1967 to a careful review of the whole range of antipoverty activities. Senator Edmund S. Muskie, Democrat of Maine, a loyal administration supporter and a man of steadily rising influence in the Senate, launched a full-scale study of the administrative jungle in which Great Society programs found themselves entrapped. In short, OEO's legislative problems were not merely those it might expect to encounter when the conservative bipartisan coalition in Congress reasserts its influence.*

The popularity of the Neighborhood Youth Corps and Project

---

*Richard Boone of the Citizens Crusade Against Poverty, testifying before Senator Clark's subcommittee investigating the antipoverty program, said on March 16, 1967, that OEO should get out of the operations field and concentrate on strengthening local community action programs.

Head Start ought to be examined. How did NYC and Head Start manage to achieve congressional popularity and enroll hundreds of thousands of individuals at the same time that other antipoverty measures, community action most notably, produced a series of administrative and political headaches? The superficial explanation is that neither NYC nor Head Start is terribly complicated in concept, but a larger part of the answer is that both provide federal funds which are used to finance projects that can readily be undertaken by almost any local public school system—*without any fundamental change in the system.* Most of the people enrolled in NYC projects are teenagers still in school; they are enrolled in what are called, simply enough, "in school" programs. Technically, Head Start is not much more complicated than an ordinary nursery school, and, in fact, is run on that basis by much the same kind of people in most communities.*

PROGRESS WITHOUT CHANGE

The Neighborhood Youth Corps and Head Start are worthy undertakings, but neither requires basic change in the system, and only rarely (as in the case of CDGM) does either challenge the status quo. Indeed, this now looms as a problem in itself. Head Start may do more harm than good unless it is connected to basic reform in the schools the children enter following the Head Start experience. A major study of Head Start by Dr. Max Wolff concluded: "Head Start cannot substitute for the long overdue improvements of education which have failed the Negro and Puerto Rican children. It can only prepare them to reap the full benefits of better education when it is provided." The Wolff study also warned that ". . . more damage is done to the child who looks forward eagerly to an educational program he has learned to enjoy than to the child who has had no previous knowledge of what to expect, if the later school is poor."[25]

Most Neighborhood Youth Corps projects find useful tasks for teenagers who need money and who surely are not damaged by the experience of working. They serve usefully as nurses' aides, library

---

*I am aware that Head Start *ought* to be much more than a nursery school, and in some instances it has been. The reference here is to the program as it appears in *most* communities.

assistants, office helpers, playground supervisors, teachers' aides, and in a variety of community projects.

Speaking in May, 1966, and reflecting on the first year and a half of program activity, Secretary of Labor Willard Wirtz reported an enrollment of 200,000 young people in the Neighborhood Youth Corps but placed the number of enrollees against a "problem area" (as he called it) of 1.7 million young Americans who seemed in need of similar help. The Secretary declared: "Part of the Neighborhood Youth Corps responsibility is to see that it leads to something else."[26] Mr. Wirtz made it clear that in his view the best answer to poverty is jobs.

Although the Neighborhood Youth Corps has done useful work, has reached its "target" population, and continues to enroll many young people, it is not yet clear how many NYC local projects relate to anything significant beyond the immediate project. At the end of 1966, only a tiny fraction of several hundred thousand NYC "alumni" had managed to find openings for further job training under the Manpower Development and Training Act, although both programs are administered by the Labor Department. The number of NYC "alumni" who were receiving on-the-job training— thought to be the most meaningful kind of training for many disadvantaged youths—was exceedingly small. In short, the education and training revolution which must take place if there is to be an effective attack on joblessness among youths, and especially among those who are non-white, had not gathered momentum as the program entered its third year.

COMMUNITY ACTION: MILDER VERSION

How President Johnson chooses to play his leadership role will profoundly affect the outcome of the struggle. In his February, 1967, message to Congress presenting a broad program for children, the President recognized the necessity of moving beyond Head Start, and requested $135 million to extend the program of pre-school training for poor children into the lower grades of elementary school. One had the feeling reading it that henceforth presidential statements would place less emphasis on the war on poverty in terms of the Economic Opportunity Act and would tend to bring OEO-sponsored programs, at least rhetorically, within a broader framework of activity. This blurring of program identity may have rather special implications for the future of community action. Community action, especially that version which includes heavy emphasis on "maximum feasible participation" of the poor, might be put aside in favor of a milder form. Once tamed, it might be rationalized as part of the model cities approach under the direction of the new Department of Housing and Urban Affairs, an agency with which mayors feel more comfortable. This, at any rate, is what many members of the community action staff at OEO headquarters feared most as the program entered its third year.

On March 14, 1967, President Johnson sent a message on urban and rural poverty to the Congress which indicated clearly the extent to which the more militant theory of community action was being supplanted by an approach which sought to conciliate mayors, governors, and congressmen. Not only were antipoverty programs to be subject to tighter administrative controls, but public officials were to be drawn more closely into planning the programs of community action groups. The presidential message stipulated: "There should be a requirement for representation of local public agencies on Community Action boards, as well as representation for the neighborhood groups to be served." All of which caused the *New Republic* to lament editorially:

> The President officially bid farewell to the original poverty program last week by asking Congress to tie local community action programs to city hall. . . . The President's latest proposals would turn the whole program into a handy patronage device. . . . What began as an attempt at fundamental change has degenerated into a joke.[27]

Herbert Krosney, in a study which is critical of the antipoverty program, quotes an anonymous "top policy official" whose views are repeated here because they have been echoed by many poverty workers at the local level:

> "Poverty is just a fad anyway. It's a gimmick. It's something everybody can be for now. But labor and business and the social welfare establishment don't have any real sympathy for the program as it is now conceived; it's something nice—so far. It doesn't threaten anybody. And as long as the program accomplished the purpose of buying off riots, or if people believe it is buying off riots, or even some minor forms of social protest,

then it's doing the job. If the poverty program becomes a real mess, Johnson will change, ever so subtly at first perhaps, until he's doing something else which isn't really today's poverty program—doing away with slums, for instance, which doesn't take involvement of the poor. This sounds like the same thing, but it isn't the same thing at all. . . ."[28]

An administration finding its freedom of action limited by a congressional majority more interested in "sound administration" and "program coordination" than in fundamental reform, and facing a public seemingly unmoved by the squalor and the degradation of the ghetto, might seek to remold community action as a means of accommodating to existing bureaucratic structures rather than continue the assignment of remaking them. Actually, many community action programs, including several reasonably effective ones, had had close working relationships with city hall at the outset, and, in that sense, the presidential message of March 14 was not quite the sell-out the *New Republic* imagined it to be.

Although the war on poverty in 1967 was obviously not the same as the war on poverty when it first took shape in 1964, the war was still being fought, as it had been since its earliest hours, on a limited scale. This was discouraging to those who wanted the war to accelerate; but a limited war seemed preferable to *no* war against poverty. Nor did the taming of community action necessarily portend the weakening of all other means of attack. The presidential message so deplored by the *New Republic* also revealed that the Johnson administration was recommending an appropriation of $135 million under the Economic Opportunity Act to train and put to work as many as 100,000 slum residents during the next fiscal year. Two days later, Secretary of Labor Wirtz, who was placed in charge of the new program, announced that the administration was prepared to use between $75 million and $90 million of uncommitted 1967 funds in order to launch this crash program aimed at rehabilitating the hard-core unemployed of the urban slums. The Wirtz program, in which OEO, HEW, and HUD were to participate jointly with the Labor Department, wisely chose to concentrate its fire first on a small group of selected cities, each with a dark ghetto—Washington, Cleveland, Chicago, Detroit, New York, Boston, St. Louis, and Los Angeles. Other cities were expected to follow later.

Unlike a number of earlier antipoverty special efforts, the Wirtz attack on ghetto unemployment was preceded by a careful survey in several major ghettos in an attempt to gain a better understanding of the nature and extent of joblessness in urban slums than is possible on the basis of the usual census and statistical data. The survey, conducted at the end of 1966, included three Negro ghettos in New York City as well as similar slums in Boston, New Orleans, Philadelphia, Phoenix, St. Louis, San Antonio, and San Francisco. The employment problems of the residents of these urban slums were found to be so much more severe than the regular monthly surveys had suggested that the Labor Department's report concluded: "No conceivable increase in the gross national product would stir these backwaters."[29]

BATTLES YET UNFOUGHT

The war on poverty cannot be passed off as a joke or a fad precisely because six years of continuous economic growth have barely stirred these backwaters. Three years of skirmishing leave the major battles to be fought. Three years after his declaration of war on poverty, President Johnson reported five and a half million children under age six, and nine million more under age seventeen, still living in families too poor to feed and house them adequately. (Nearly two out of every three disadvantaged children between the ages of five and fourteen had *never* visited a dentist.) Five million of the elderly poor in 1967 awaited a fundamental strengthening of the social security system, as proposed by the Johnson administration. As many as 7,400,000 Americans—three and a half million of them children—were somehow struggling along on the miserable basis which public assistance payments provided, despite the extremely critical report of the Advisory Council on Public Welfare (June, 1966) which found these payments ". . ."so low and so uneven that the Government is, by its own standards and definitions, a major source of the poverty on which it has declared unconditional war."

If the Johnson administration seemed a trifle reluctant at times to face the harsh realities of the politics of poverty, it had been more forthright than any administration since FDR in presenting the sobering facts about poverty. The Johnson administration also moved far beyond any recent administration in the scope of its health, education, and welfare programs, and funded them far more generously. The Johnson administration showed greater willingness to experiment with new techniques of social action than any national administration since the New Deal. No president, including Abraham Lincoln, went as far as Lyndon Johnson had gone in pledging presidential support to the cause of Negro equality in America.

The tragedy is that our obsession with Vietnam absorbed presidential attention and distorted all of this, and, as a result, national priorities shifted between 1964–65 and 1966–67 far more than most Americans seem to realize. James Reston ably summarized the status of the war on poverty as it entered the third year: "The problem is defined; the programs all have vivid names; the machinery, new and still imperfect, is nevertheless in place; but the funds are lamentably inadequate to the gigantic scope of the problem."[30]

Furthermore, the President's almost total preoccupation with Vietnam came at a time when he ought to have been giving maximum attention to his own "power stakes" in the war on poverty. Presidential leadership depends upon the careful nurturing of presidential power. In 1967 the Johnson administration faced this prospect: if the administration succeeded in placating most of the "regular" politicians and bureaucrats who wanted to resist or limit an effective attack on poverty, it would undoubtedly also succeed in exacerbating the deep bitterness which pervaded the nation's ghettos. Despair among young Negroes mounted as the overly advertised poverty war failed to change the conditions of their lives. The danger of a series of violent explosions far worse than any the nation had yet seen was very great by the summer of 1967.

Although the war on poverty remained a limited effort, in part because the President's attention (and large federal appropriations) had been diverted to Southeast Asia, there was reason to assume that a cessation of hostilities in Vietnam would probably cause the Johnson administration to attempt frantically to escalate the war on poverty as part of a broader effort to keep the economy from tail-spinning into a serious recession. Whether the Johnson administration would have the capacity to seize the initiative once again in the congressional arena and push forward effectively on issues of social reform seemed doubtful, however. The program suffered from a growing impression of widespread administrative inadequacies. Congress increasingly found it difficult to identify itself with a program it had done so little to create. Some congressional liberals as well as conservatives now viewed the antipoverty program as being, on balance, a rather confusing mixture of administrative problems and political ambiguities. And, not least important, the war on poverty represented a major program of social reform which lacked widespread popular support and understanding. Most of the people who might be helped by a war on poverty exist outside the usual boundaries of American politics and American political discourse. They inhabit the "Other America." Whether they also exist outside the conscience of the rest of America remains to be seen.

CHAPTER 9

STALEMATE ON THE DOMESTIC FRONT, 1967-1972

"The question is, which war is more important at this particular time? We have had poverty always. We will always have it. . . ."

REP. GEORGE MAHON, CHAIRMAN
House Committee on Appropriations
October, 1966

THE MOST NOTEWORTHY aspect of the Economic Opportunity Act has been a capacity for survival in the face of official indifference, congressional debate, presidential neglect, bureaucratic in-fighting, and a fair amount of cynicism at the grass roots. President Johnson's war against poverty was the first domestic program casualty resulting from the policy of military escalation in Vietnam, 1965–1968, and yet, the act and all of its programs were functioning and being fought over in 1972. The original decisions to hold back the attack against poverty were taken in 1966; they were reflected first in the budget which the Johnson administration submitted for fiscal year 1967. Every one of the important programs sanctioned by the act managed to survive the budgetary squeeze, even after the administrative responsibility was transferred in 1969 to a Republican administration which had no natural affinity for the antipoverty activities it had inherited from the mid-1960s. The Economic Opportunity Act, brought forth in 1964 as a prime piece of presidential legislation, written in the first instance within the Johnson White House, conspicuously bearing the LBJ label, won the grudging and largely passive support of the Nixon administration. The Job Corps, an early favorite of Sargent Shriver, the first OEO director, was the only program casualty during the 1969–1972 period, and it proved to be a partial casualty. While the Nixon administration took the action which drastically altered and limited the nature of the Job Corps activity, it is a near certainty that a Democratic president, following Johnson, would have found it expedient to have followed much the same course. The Job Corps was in serious trouble—political, administrative, congressional—long before the election of 1968 was decided. The fact that the Economic Opportunity Act, including a remodeled Job Corps, survived during the first four Nixon years tells something about the essentially incremental nature of public policy-making at the national level.[1]

The Economic Opportunity Act, viewed from the same perspective in the early 1970s, affords interesting insights into the role of Congress in domestic policy making. The act, we recall, moved through both houses of Congress to its original enactment in August, 1964, with unusual ease. As an important item of presidential legislation brought before the Congress in a national election year, the act naturally encountered disciplined resistance on the part of the Republican congressional minority. However, skillful legislative leadership, emanating from the White House, succeeded in winning over some sixty Southern Democratic congressmen who joined with Representative Phil Landrum, Democrat of Georgia, the bill's floor manager, in putting together a majority in favor of Lyndon B. Johnson's war against poverty. Such an unusual degree of congressional acceptance of presidentially-initiated social reform legislation could not have been expected to last indefinitely. As noted in earlier chapters, the congressional resistance built up first within the Appropriations committees, but the tendency for Congress to play a stronger and, occasionally, a more critical role also exhibited itself in the substantive committees of the House and Senate. As the congressional committees came to exert more detailed control over both the substance and the program funds, they also developed definite program biases. Thus, the Job Corps became vulnerable, at least in part, because the congressional committees overseeing the antipoverty program came to believe that the Job Corps was unduly expensive while producing results which were often disappointing. By way of contrast, congressional committees also soon developed favorite programs, the Neighborhood Youth Corps and Head Start being only the two most obvious examples. There were reasons for this, one feels certain. NYC and Head Start shared the advantage that either one could be undertaken in almost any community without necessarily requiring fundamental change in existing political and bureaucratic structures. By 1966–67, many congressmen had "successful" NYC and Head Start projects in their home districts.

Furthermore, Congress, through its appropriate committees, soon developed its own technical expertise in those program areas funded under the Economic Opportunity Act. Legislative spokesmen such as Senators Joseph Clark and Gaylord Nelson, Representatives James O'Hara, Carl Perkins, John Brademas, and Edith Green, all Democrats, and Senator Jacob Javits and Representative Albert Quie on the Republican side gained various degrees of technical competence in this general area. More than this, especially in the House where each representative has but one committee, these same legislators (and others as well) understood that their careers in Congress and their political reputations at home depended to some degree on the "effectiveness" of the programs they were helping to shape. In short, Congress, slowly and a little reluctantly at first, developed *its own stake* in the programs authorized by the Economic Opportunity Act.

When Richard M. Nixon came to the White House following a relatively narrow popular victory in November, 1968, a victory which left him as a "plurality" president facing Democratic majorities in both houses of Congress, he was to find that the Economic Opportunity Act enjoyed a kind of bipartisan support in the Congress which was relatively broad albeit not very deep. The act was no longer simply an LBJ program of social reform. President Johnson who had succumbed to his own obsession with Vietnam had long since abandoned the antipoverty program to its own fate. There was also a real question in 1968 as to how much of the social-reform impetus was left in what had originally been called the *war* on poverty. Having been "tamed," the program had gained the same kind of generalized congressional support which had also attended the manpower training programs since the early 1960s. Indeed, several of the Economic Opportunity Act programs were seen as being part of the manpower-training complex.

The incremental nature of the federal budgetary process also tended to keep the antipoverty program alive. How does one turn off a set of programs which annually pump two billion dollars into thousands of local projects? Aaron Wildavsky in his pioneering study of the politics of the budgetary process made the point with clarity and simplicity when he noted that the largest single factor in this year's budget is last year's budget.[2] This aspect is clearly revealed in the budgetary experience of the Economic Opportunity Act between 1967 and 1972, an important part of the subsequent analysis in this chapter. Budgetary incrementalism relates directly to bureaucratic momentum (i.e., the tendency in large organizations to keep on doing what they have been doing). Pressures were building up within the Congress during the Johnson years to move operating programs out of the Office of Economic Opportunity, an agency of the institutionalized presidency, and to place them in the appropriate cabinet departments. It was left to the Nixon administration to carry out this process of administrative devolution. Nixon's OEO was destined to become a unit for planning and evaluation.

In terms of survival, there was at least one advantage when a program moved from OEO to an established department; the antipoverty program became part of an on-going departmental program; the antipoverty bureaucracy became a sub-unit within a larger, well-established bureaucracy; it became part of the on-going bureaucratic process, a process which is seldom reversed and then only with great difficulty. When Head Start was moved to the Department of Health, Education, and Welfare in 1969 there was the possibility that innovating zeal might suffer somewhat in the transfer, but offsetting this was the assumption that henceforth Head Start would enjoy some of the benefit of HEW's not inconsiderable lobbying power, assuming the bureaucratic overlords of HEW were not averse, as apparently they were not, to having still another large operating program added to HEW's rapidly expanding empire. The same process appears to have been at work in the case of the Job Corps which was transferred to the Labor Department's Manpower Administration in 1969. At first, the program was altered in substance while funds and enrollments were cut back sharply; then in fiscal 1972 the Nixon administration increased the Job Corps budget again in order to *add* 20 large residential centers and 7 smaller ones with a total enrollment of 5,100 youths. With a bit of luck, the Job Corps may go on forever, in the fashion of the Bureau of Apprenticeship and Training.

Nothing touched upon in this chapter should divert attention from a crucial fact: as the Economic Opportunity programs, one by one, gained broad congressional acceptance, became enmeshed in the incremental process of annual budget making, and were increasingly institutionalized within the departmental bureaucratic structures, they were "tamed" politically and administratively. The process of homogenization rendered the antipoverty programs more "acceptable" in the circles of orthodoxy. This process was well underway when the original edition of this book first appeared in 1967. The mayors were the first to react when community action and the "maximum feasible participation" corollary seemed to threaten their established local power bases, just as the mayors, including Chicago's Richard Daley, had been among the first to support the act in its early hours when the lure of federal dollars seemed stronger than the reality of federal muscle and federal reformist zeal. Before Richard Nixon succeeded Lyndon Johnson as President, it would have been difficult to find a big city mayor who felt much threatened by activities sponsored by the Economic Opportunity Act. To the contrary, most mayors in the late 1960s and the early 1970s were seeking additional antipoverty funds. In the next chapter more attention will be given to the longer-range significance which community action programs have had across the nation.

PUTTING THE BRAKES ON

The first effective curb was placed upon the expansion of the antipoverty program in 1966. The brakes were applied first within the agencies of the institutionalized presidency during the preparation of President Johnson's budget for fiscal 1967. The signal could only have come from the White House for the Bureau of the Budget to have done what was done to Sargent Shriver's request for funds. As we shall soon see, his request was cut in half by the Budget Bureau in December 1965–January 1966, following the first year of military escalation in Vietnam. Since Congress was not likely to increase the presidential level of spending for a presidential domestic program at a time when military spending was threatening to soar out of control, thanks to the Americanization of the war in Vietnam, fiscal 1967 was a critical year in the budgetary life of OEO. The fact that it was the White House which initiated the drastic cut in the expansion of Shriver's program was established definitively in hearings held by the House Appropriations Subcommittee chaired by Representative John Fogarty, Democrat of Rhode Island, in October, 1966.

The subcommittee had been in session only a short time on Monday, October 3, 1966, when the following exchange took place between Sargent Shriver, the director of OEO, and the subcommittee chairman:

> Mr. Fogarty: "Are you better prepared than you were last year to tell us how your original proposals to the Bureau of the Budget vary from what is included in the President's budget? I had a tough time getting this out of you last year."
>
> Mr. Shriver: "We have to get permission to get that figure."
>
> Mr. Fogarty: "I do not care where you get it, but you can leave the room and the hearing is concluded if you don't get it. Do I get through to you?"
>
> Mr. Shriver: "Yes, sir."
>
> Mr. Kelly: "$3.4 billion."[3]

The alacrity with which Mr. Kelly supplied the information which Shriver seemed unwilling to give the powerful chairman of the House Appropriations Subcommittee bears further comment. Shriver, a presidential appointee serving as head of the program, was following the protocol of appropriations politics. He was bound, at least in theory, not to reveal the administratively confidential point that it was the White House and the Budget Bureau which had cut his request for funds in half long before Congress had had any opportunity to work its will. William Kelly, the OEO budget director, was an experienced civil servant. He was less vulnerable than Shriver to White House-imposed sanctions. Kelly was also technically and bureaucratically sophisticated enough to realize that this was no time to dally with so tough and determined an Appropriations Subcommittee chairman as John Fogarty.[4] Fogarty, for his part, presumably was intent on underlining the basic political point that the initial decision to hold the war on poverty within budgetary limits previously established (that is, to keep it from normal expansion), was a presidential, not a congressional, decision. OEO's original request for funds had been cut in half no later than January, 1966. It seems clear that Fogarty wanted the record of his subcommittee to show that whatever might happen in the House by way of imposing fiscal limitations on the antipoverty program would be minor and marginal when compared with the limits President Johnson had already placed upon his own program.

Fogarty and his colleagues on the subcommittee were also interested in establishing the effect a $1.75 billion appropriation rather than the $3.4 billion OEO had requested would have upon each of the principal programs. Through judicious questioning, the Appropriations Subcommittee determined that the Bureau had reduced the Neighborhood Youth Corps request from $600 million to approximately $300 million in fiscal 1967. In a similar fashion, testimony revealed that community action funds had been trimmed from $1.4 billion in the original OEO request to $900 million in the president's budget. The subcommittee also learned that $2 billion would have been closer to what the community action planners would have preferred.[5]

HALF THE BULLETS

The same House Appropriations Subcommittee hearings in October, 1966, were attended part of the time by Rep. George Mahon, Democrat of Texas, the chairman of the parent committee. The following exchange between Mahon, a senior congressional oligarch, and Shriver, heading the presidential war on poverty, suggests the sense of priorities which prevailed in the Congress in the midst of the American military escalation in Vietnam:[6]

Mr. Mahon: "Mr. Shriver, I heard your testimony yesterday and I was looking it over this afternoon for the purpose of ascertaining your comments as to the adequacy of the budget. I believe that you said that you had to have at least this $1.750 million, in order to do the sort of job you wanted to do.

I would like to feel that regardless of the amount of money provided by Congress, and we have no way of telling what it will be, that you would do the most creditable job possible with the funds made available. Is that correct?"

Mr. Shriver: "Yes sir. There is no question about that. We will do the best we can."

Next Chairman Mahon wanted to know why OEO should not continue operating at the level of $1.5 billion, the limit established for fiscal 1966.

Mr. Mahon: "I would like to think that within the framework of whatever figure is given you, you could give some here and take some there and administer a program for $1.5 billion that ought to be pretty effective. I mean if you could not accomplish a lot of good with $1.5 billion there would be something wrong."

Mr. Shriver: "It is not that you cannot do a lot of good with 1.5 billion dollars. . . . As you say, these things are all a matter of relativity. You said it does not make any difference whether it is $1.5 billion, $1.75 billion, the budget figure is not the important thing."

Having just reminded Shriver that fiscal 1967 budget was a budget for "troubled times," Mahon remarked at one point in the dialogue, "And of course there are certain priorities which have to be taken into consideration."

Shriver finally saw an opportunity to state the problem in a manner which might seem familiar to Mahon who had long been chairman of the House Appropriations Subcommittee handling the military budget:

Mr. Shriver: "It is a little bit like the priority if you are fighting a war. In the war, you do send, as the president frequently says to General Westmoreland, what he needs to win the war. It is not that he could not do a good job with half the number of bullets. We will do what we can with half the bullets. But this is not, on the other hand, to say that we can do what needs to be done in this war with half the ammunition."

Mr. Mahon: "Yes, but you do not think you can do it with $1.750 million. You think you need $3.2 billion. . . . The question is, which war is more important at this particular time? We have had poverty always. We will always have it. . . ."

Thus having paid tribute to the spirit of William Graham Sumner, Representative George Mahon of Lubbock, Texas, chairman of the powerful House Appropriations Committee, signaled Sargent Shriver that the congressional appropriations process would ratify the decisions made in January by President Johnson and his budget advisers; the war on poverty would not expand in fiscal year 1967 because the war in Vietnam held a higher priority.* George Mahon presided over the House Appropriations process during the entire period of escalation in Vietnam. He apparently experienced no difficulty in approving expenditures exceeding $128 billion for the war in Vietnam during fiscal years 1965 to 1972.[7] The so-called war against poverty was granted about $15.5 billion during the same period. There is no question about the relative priorities as perceived within the institutionalized presidency and the conservative congressional coalition.[8]

1967—BOSSES AND BOLL WEEVILS

President Johnson probably ignored the ironic symbolism as he signed the bill, S. 2388, providing a two-year authorization for the antipoverty program two days before Christmas 1967 while en route from Cam Ranh Bay, South Vietnam, to Karachi, Pakistan. Nonetheless, the enactment of the bill (Public Law 90–222) represented a victory for the White House after a struggle in which it had seemed for a time that the House might kill the program. Instead, the war on poverty emerged at the end of 1967 "remarkably intact," as *The Congressional Quarterly* later observed. In addition to extending the program authority for two more years, Congress voted a $1.773 billion appropriation for fiscal 1968, thus continuing OEO programs at approximately the fiscal 1967 level.[9]

The Republican members of the House Committee on Labor and Education challenged the Johnson administration by offering their own proposal, the "Opportunity Crusade," calling for the abolition of OEO and the transfer of all OEO-run programs to the regular

---

*Lyndon B. Johnson fails to mention this vital point in his memoirs, *The Vantage Point* (New York, 1971). His chapter on the war on poverty is selective, superficial, and self-defensive.

departments. Although urban riots in July and August did nothing to improve the atmosphere in the House where the antipoverty program was under heavy attack, a strong effort in support of the program was centered in the Senate Committee on Labor and Public Welfare. Finally, the antipoverty program was saved, in effect, by the so-called Green amendment requiring that all local community action funds be channeled through and controlled by public officials. The amendment which was put forward at an open meeting of the House committee in October by Representative Edith Green, Democrat of Oregon, had the effect of making the program more acceptable to some of the Southern Democratic representatives while solidifying support among big city Democrats. The Green amendment also seems to have helped in taking some of the steam out of the Republican effort to "spin-off" OEO programs to the departments. When House Republican orators referred to Mrs. Green's proposal as "the bosses and boll weevil" amendment, the Opportunity Crusade lost some of the allure it might otherwise have had for Southern Democratic legislators. The bill with the Green amendment passed the House on November 15, 1967, without any other major change and without any of the Republican spin-off proposals.

When the Senate Committee on Labor and Public Welfare sent S. 2388 to the floor on September 12, the committee report accompanying the bill (S. Rept. 363), noted that there were still nearly 30 million Americans living in conditions of poverty. The committee report observed that ". . . the poverty program, because it has never been funded at a level commensurate with needs, at its best is barely scratching the surface of community relations, and the remedies will be far costlier and much more difficult than the limited efforts so far underway." At the same time, the committee recommended a new $2.5 billion job program, saying that the hearings had shown "a clear consensus . . . that jobs are the single most effective way to combat poverty."[10] If so, the President and the Congress ignored this "clear consensus."

1968—A LULL IN THE FIGHTING

The year which featured presidential abdication, an apparent reversal of the official course in Vietnam, the McCarthy and Kennedy challenges, two senseless assassinations, the violent and volatile Democratic National Convention in Chicago, and the election of Richard M. Nixon as the next President, proved to be a strangely uneventful period in the life of the antipoverty program. Congress had done whatever it wished to do the previous year, and the people responsible for administering the war on poverty seemed content to have public attention focused elsewhere. The Congress appropriated almost $2 billion for all OEO-run programs in fiscal 1969, representing the highest appropriation in the history of the program.[11]

1969–THE NIXON ADMINISTRATION TAKES OVER

Political realism might have predicted the demise of the Economic Opportunity Act in 1969; the program's authorization was due to expire on June 30 and the new Republican President owed little to Lyndon Johnson's version of social reform. Nevertheless, in his first message to Congress (February 19) President Nixon recommended a one-year extension of the antipoverty program; later in the year, he was to change this, asking for a two-year extension. On April 9, the President announced the transfer of the Head Start program to a new Office of Child Development in HEW. Robert Finch, the secretary of HEW and a close political associate of the president, said that Head Start programs on a year-round basis were to be expanded while summer programs would be reduced. Two days later George P. Schultz, the secretary of labor, announced the closing of fifty-nine Job Corps centers; thirty new nonresidential urban centers were to be established to train unskilled young people. Representative Donald Rumsfeld, Republican of Illinois, was appointed director of OEO on April 21. He was to reorganize OEO as a planning and research unit and as the initiator of experimental programs; the long established operating programs were being moved to the departments.

The future of the OEO programs remained in some doubt throughout most of the year, especially in the House where the bill authorizing a two-year extension did not reach the House floor until December. Turning back a determined Republican-Southern Democratic effort aimed at transferring the antipoverty program to the states, Congress finally passed a bill (S. 3016) on December 20 extending the program *unchanged* for two more years. In a confusing parliamentary situation, the Senate three days earlier had voted an appropriation of $2.048 billion for the program. After a conference committee had reduced the figure to $1.948 billion, Congress adjourned for the holidays without completing action on a final appropriation. Caught in a struggle between the White House and Congress over funds for HEW and the Labor Department, the OEO appropriation for fiscal 1970 did not clear Congress until March 4, 1970, with only about a third of the fiscal year remaining. It was hardly an inspiring way to live, but the Economic Opportunity Act had survived the first year of a Republican administration.[12]

1970—BEHIND THE SCENES STRUGGLE

No important floor battles directly involving OEO were fought in 1970, the second Nixon year. In that sense, it was one of the quieter years for the antipoverty program. Behind the scenes activity, however, forewarned of an intense struggle ahead. There were indications that the program would probably have to battle for its life in Congress in 1971. Democratic leaders of the House and Senate committees feared that Donald Rumsfeld had been appointed director of OEO precisely in order to preside over the liquidation of an empire, although Rumsfeld was vehement in denying the charge.

One of the most momentous backstage struggles concerned the organization and the future role of the Legal Services Office whose program was widely regarded as one of the most effective of the antipoverty activities. The program operated through 850 neighborhood law offices in 265 communities in 49 of the 50 states. There were 1800 full-time staff attorneys in the Legal Services system representing a potent new force on the side of poor people. Rumsfeld, in a 1969 reorganization, took Legal Services out of the Community Action Division and established the Office of Legal Services as a separate organization reporting to the director of OEO. The reasons given were to provide recognition for the program and to provide a focus within OEO on the mission of being an advocate for the poor.

The Legal Services program claimed to be serving some two

million clients. Rather than concentrate simply on a case-by-case approach, "the poverty lawyers" used test cases and class action suits challenging laws and administrative regulations affecting large numbers of poor people.[13] In one instance, the California Rural Legal Assistance group brought a class action suit restoring $210 million in medical service for a million and a half persons which Governor Ronald Reagan's administration had tried to cut from the state budget. In turn, California Republican Senator George Murphy introduced an amendment which would have given governors veto power over specific Legal Services projects in their states. The Senate accepted the so-called Murphy amendment in October, 1969. Donald Rumsfeld fought against the amendment as did the American Bar Association, and it was dropped from the bill in its final form.

The issue did not die as the struggle intensified within OEO. At one point it was learned that Rumsfeld was giving serious consideration to a proposal which would have placed Legal Services activities in the field under the regional directors of OEO. Terry Lenzer, the head of Legal Services, resisted the proposal on the grounds that the professionalism of the "poverty lawyers" would be hopelessly compromised if their projects had to be cleared with the political and bureaucratic "realists" serving as OEO regional directors. Leading Democrats on the substantive congressional committees were known to be in sympathy with Lenzer. The internal struggle continued until December. Finally, Rumsfeld tabled the proposal; he also fired Lenzer.[14]

An OEO experiment in state control over an antipoverty program posed another troublesome issue. During House floor debate in December, 1969, Representative Edith Green, Democrat of Oregon, and Representative Albert H. Quie, Republican of Minnesota, offered a substitute bill which would have turned over the control of the antipoverty programs to the states. The so-called "Quie-Green" amendment was defeated in a 163–231 roll call vote. Consequently, a number of key Democrats on the House Labor and Education Committee were distinctly unhappy to learn a few months later that OEO was planning to try an experimental state-run program in Oklahoma. Their argument in protest was that the agency was doing administratively that which Congress had just voted should not be done. The Oklahoma project was based on a demonstration grant of $466,000; applications for community action programs at the local level were processed by the state to determine whether they should be forwarded to the regional office of OEO for final approval. In this manner, a kind of administrative veto was placed in the hands of the state agency. After receiving the objections of congressional Democrats, OEO let it be known that the same plan would not be tried in other states.

The Oklahoma project "demonstrated" basic philosophic differences between Rumsfeld and those congressional Democrats who were friendly toward the earlier version of the war on poverty. While Rumsfeld's OEO saw value in giving state officials a more substantial role in the program, the Democrats perceived in the Legal Services struggle and the Oklahoma project, to say nothing of the administrative "spin-off" of antipoverty programs into the old-line established bureaucracies, a continuing trend aimed at weakening the community action features of the Economic Opportunity Act.[15]

1971–PRESIDENT VERSUS CONGRESS VERSUS CHILDREN

The bitter struggle between President and Congress over the future of the program, long predicted, finally broke into the open in 1971 during President Nixon's third year in office. Both sides favored a two-year extension of the program while differing sharply on matters of substance, size, shape, and scope. The differences were substantial enough to culminate in a presidential veto in December.

The battle was joined early during hearings which the House Labor and Education Committee held in March. The hearings opened with leading Democrats charging the Nixon administration with seeking to dismantle the antipoverty program under the guise of administrative reorganization. Technically, the administration's position was impeccable: the President was asking Congress for another two-year extension of the program whose legal and fiscal authority was due to expire on June 30. On the other hand, the President's critics in the Congress reasoned that his revenue sharing proposals when combined with his reorganization plans would have the practical effect of transferring, merging, or eliminating a number of OEO's functions.

Representative Augustus F. Hawkins, Democrat of California, asked Frank Carlucci, the acting director of OEO:

Why don't you say what you're doing? You're dismantling OEO, stripping it of all its programs, and there won't be any agency to coordinate the programs for the poor.

Carlucci insisted that the placing of certain programs in the departments did not imply a diminished concern for the clients being served.

"I prefer to look at the programs and not the institutions," he said. "The programs have been important to the poor—and they have been strengthened." [16]

Thus, the Nixon administration argued before the Congress in 1971 in support of the antipoverty program on the basis that a Republican administration was prepared to administer the so-called war on poverty more efficiently than the original Democratic sponsors had been able to do. Congressional Democrats, not to be outdone by the Nixon administration in devotion to the program, produced a bill which went considerably beyond the limits the White House had in mind for a prudent effort. The Senate passed the bill (S. 2007) on September 9, after a vigorous Republican effort to drop a two-billion-dollar comprehensive child care program failed. Building upon the generally favorable congressional disposition toward Head Start, committee Democrats in the Senate had added a major new program calling for a broad range of educational, nutritional, and health standards for children from families classified as having a "poverty" living standard. The House passed its version (H.R. 10351) on September 30 by a margin of 251 to 115. While differing from the Senate bill in a number of details, the House bill was amended on the floor so as to include essentially the same child development provisions which the White House had opposed in the Senate.

After the inevitable conference committee had ironed out the differences between House and Senate versions of the antipoverty bill, both houses voted to adopt the conference report. The Senate voted its acceptance by a margin of 63–17 (7 Southern Democrats and 10 Republicans opposing) on December 2. The House voted 210–187 in favor of the bill containing the two-billion-dollar child care program and the two-year extension. 135 House Republicans voted in opposition. Two days later the President vetoed the bill calling the child development program "the most deeply flawed provision of this legislation." The veto message indicated White House disapproval of certain details of the Legal Services Corporation which the bill would have created. The President also took exception to language in the bill limiting Executive authority to effect future transfers of programs to the departments. But there was little doubt that it was mainly the child care issue which had provoked the veto.

The Senate failed to override the president's veto. The vote taken on December 10 was 51–36, 7 short of the necessary two-thirds.[17]

Thus 1971 ended with the legal and fiscal future of the antipoverty program uncertain.

1972–IN THE VETO'S AFTERMATH

In the course of the congressional debate and an intensive White House lobbying effort, it became clear that President Nixon had at least two objections to the comprehensive child development feature as an addition to the antipoverty program. The President's number one domestic priority was welfare reform as contained in H.R. 1 which the House had passed on June 22, 1971. H.R. 1 included a $750 million authorization for day care service and the construction of day care facilities. This program was targeted at children whose parents were required to register for work or training. In short, the president felt that the more comprehensive child development program in the Economic Opportunity Act might lessen support for his own "manpower" version of child care. Perhaps equally important, the congressional version of child development as written into the antipoverty bill carried an expensive price tag. The Nixon administration had no taste for an additional two-billion-dollar program aimed at assisting pre-school children in fiscal 1972–1973.

This time the congressional Democrats decided to bring forth a bill which would not include comprehensive child care. Once again the Nixon administration offered objections. Certain provisions relating to legal services, child care, and Head Start were still troubling the White House. Philip V. Sanchez, who had been appointed director of OEO only one day before hearings opened in the House committee in January, found his official honeymoon extraordinarily brief. Speaking of the new version the committee had just put together following the veto, Sanchez told the House committee:

> This measure does not conform with the Administration's recommendation that the authorities [sic] of the Economic Opportunity Act be extended without amendment and it contains provisions which are undesirable.

Representative John Brademas, Democrat of Indiana, the prime sponsor of the child development proposal in the previous legislative session, a proposal which had been eliminated in accordance with White House wishes, retorted:

> Some of you down there want to abolish Congress so you can get your job done. It does seem to me that some of the people in this Administration ought to pay more attention to the Founding Fathers and realize there are three branches of Government.

Representative Carl D. Perkins, Democrat of Kentucky, noted for qualities of patience and persistence, put the question tactfully:

> You don't expect anyone to think that a bill as complex and controversial as this one can get through Congress without amendment?

Mr. Sanchez said that the administration was opposed to certain provisions of the bill relating to the national Legal Services Corporation. The administration wanted a board of directors appointed by the president whereas the House version provided for an independent board. The White House also objected to the authorization of $500 million in fiscal 1972 and one billion in fiscal 1973 for Head Start. Mr. Sanchez stuck to the technical point that child care was dealt with more appropriately in welfare reform legislation. In the meantime, welfare reform was making its way only very slowly through the congressional labyrinth four years after its original White House launching, a situation which seemed not to bother Mr. Sanchez nor to impress the committee Democrats.[18]

The House Committee on Labor and Education reported a bill (H.R. 12350–H. Rept. 92–815) on February 4, 1972, extending the antipoverty program for two years through fiscal 1973. The vote in committee was 25 to 6 in favor of the bill. It extended the authority of those programs still administered by OEO, as well as Head Start administered by HEW and a variety of manpower training programs administered by the Labor Department, including the Neighborhood Youth Corps and the Job Corps. The extension also covered VISTA which had been transferred out of OEO to the new ACTION agency. The bill authorized expenditures totalling $2.3 billion in fiscal 1972 and $3 billion in fiscal 1973. In effect, the House committee proposed increasing antipoverty spending by approximately a third in fiscal 1973, a prospect not likely to appeal greatly to the Nixon administration which was facing a massive budget deficit.[19]

The House of Representatives passed H.R. 12350 on February 17 by a vote of 234–127. Despite the nearly two-to-one margin in favor of the new version of the two-year extension, the Nixon administration was opposed to the bill as passed.[20]

The Senate Labor and Public Welfare Committee reported two bills on May 16; S. 3010 would extend programs administered by OEO and S. 3617 would establish a child development program based on the Head Start program.[21]

The bill reported by the Senate committee by a vote of 17–0 would extend OEO's authority for three years through fiscal 1974. It authorized expenditures of $3.05 billion for fiscal 1972, $3.32 billion for fiscal 1973, and $3.32 for fiscal 1974. Since fiscal 1972 would have terminated before Congress had voted final action on the authorization, the figures authorized by the Senate committee had a certain illusory quality. At the same time the committee reported a separate bill (S. 3617) to strengthen and expand Head Start and to establish a child development program. The committee authorized expenditures of $2.95 billion in fiscal years 1973–75 to carry out the child development program as well as a proposed $500 million annual expansion of the Neighborhood Youth Corps.[22]

The Senate passed S. 3010 extending OEO for three years through fiscal 1974 by a 75–13 roll call vote on June 29. The bill authorized expenditures totaling $9.6 billion over the three-year period. Earlier, on June 20, the Senate passed a separate Head Start and child care bill, S. 3617 authorizing $2.95 billion for fiscal years 1973–75. The roll call vote was by a margin of 73–12.

Congress finally sent the President a bill (H.R. 12350) on September 5, extending OEO's authority through fiscal 1974 and authorizing expenditures of $2.36 billion in fiscal 1973 and $2.39 billion in fiscal 1974 for antipoverty programs. Final action came when the Senate by voice vote and the House by a 223–97 roll call vote approved a revised conference report on the bill which deleted a provision, originally approved by both houses, establishing an independent National Legal Services corporation. The conferees had deleted the provision apparently to avoid a threatened presidential veto. Thus, the legal services program would continue to operate within OEO. Two weeks later President Nixon signed the bill into law.[23]

Thus the nation approached a vital election which was to determine who was to provide Executive leadership during the critical middle years of the 1970s. Our analysis of the struggle between the White House and the Congress in the 1967–1972 period suggests the importance of the 1972 election in influencing the future of a number of antipoverty programs. The presidential campaign of 1972 opened with a solid cluster of antipoverty programs still in operation, a residue from an earlier period. The antipoverty program, initiated by Lyndon Johnson before escalation in Vietnam, had survived the decade despite a change in national administrations following the 1968 election. This chapter has shown that the survival of the program had come at a price; still the survival remained a remarkable fact, quite apart from the question of program effectiveness. The Economic Opportunity Act of 1964, conceived in the White House during the early hours of the Johnson administration and formulated by a task force of political technicians (JFK variety), was in its origins a prime example of presidential legislation. As we have noted previously, Congress simply ratified the act in 1964 after a cursory initial review of a bill written within the institutionalized presidency. This was a most untypical approach for Congress to adopt in addressing itself to a major legislative proposal for domestic reform. Indeed, it raised questions about the "staying power" of a controversial domestic program in whose creation Congress had played such a small part.

The first edition of this book warned about the danger of burying Congress prematurely. The congressional role in the making of domestic legislation is not a minor one. But who would have imagined in 1966–1967 that the time was near at hand when a congressional majority would identify closely with the antipoverty program? Who would have predicted in the mid-1960s that a congressional majority would soon be engaged in a prolonged struggle with a Republican President over the shape and scope of the nation's antipoverty activities, neither apparently being willing to let the program die?

CHAPTER 10

THE RHETORIC OF REFORM

> "No movement of reform in American society can hope
> to supplant the conflicts of interest from which policy
> emerges. It can only serve as advocate, not as judge."
>
> PETER MARRIS AND MARTIN REIN,
> *Dilemmas of Social Reform* (1967)

THERE HAS BEEN no completely objective evaluation of the Economic Opportunity Act nor is there likely to be one in the foreseeable future. A number of the most valuable studies have been written by participant-observers who have strong personal views about the program. The act and the programs it authorizes have meant different things to diverse participants, and views change as the program is altered and modified. There is, however, a central dilemma of the poverty program embedded in the concepts on which the program is based. James Sundquist, who served on the original Shriver task force, a man of balance and judgment, whose scholarly work shows a detailed knowledge of recent domestic programs, has posed the dilemma as well as anyone:

What was unsettled, essentially, was the issue that had been defined in the long debate on the strategy for combatting juvenile delinquency. In the war on poverty, as in the war on youth crime, was the target the individual or the community? Could poverty be eliminated by providing opportunity, or resources, to the individual within the existing "social setting" in Cloward and

162

Ohlin's phrase, or was it necessary to alter that setting, as they concluded, to heal the "sick community," to shatter and remake the "culture of poverty?"[1]

The essential dilemma persisted, unresolved, throughout the tangled legislative and administrative history of the program. Every serious attempt to evaluate the program touches upon this dilemma while coming to conclusions which often conflict with other equally important studies. Three evaluations of the antipoverty program appeared in 1969, each written by an eminent social scientist who had been close to the program. Sar Levitan, supported by a substantial Ford Foundation grant, offered an analysis, often in considerable detail, of each of the major antipoverty programs; his data in most cases included fiscal year 1968, but nothing beyond 1968.[2] Daniel P. Moynihan's book-length critique of community action[3] is chiefly helpful in sorting out the conflicting versions of community action which dominated the early history of the program. Kenneth B. Clark's study[4] which also focuses on the Community Action Program is based upon data drawn mainly from a dozen major cities during the first two years of operation. It is, in this sense, a limited evaluation. Nevertheless, Clark's assessment is the most searching of the three because he relates the dilemma to the ambiguous nature of the so-called war on poverty.

Levitan manages to strike a stance which straddles the main issue. After describing the program's principal thrust as being essentially one based upon "self-help," he finds that the act seeks ". . . to remedy the causes of poverty rather than merely to mitigate its symptoms."[5] It is not clear how the most disadvantaged members of society, many of them children, would remedy the causes of poverty through self-help methods. Nor is it easy to reconcile Levitan's acknowledgement that the program by-passes many poor people who could not benefit from self-help with the notion that the program aims at remedying causes. He also notes that the program has failed to reach many of the poor because of limited funds. On specific programs, Levitan tends to shy away from offering hard judgments on the grounds that for many of them ". . . it is simply too early for meaningful data to have been assembled."[6] Among his more important general findings: "There is little evidence that the American people are willing to assign a top priority to a real war on poverty."[7] "Poverty has not been eliminated. Society has not been restructured. And clearly the 'total war' has died aborning."[8]

Moynihan turns harsh critic of the program he helped to shape in its earliest hours. His criticism carries the suggestion, at least implicitly, that he and a number of his colleagues on the original Shriver task force were unperceptive participants in an incipient sell-out. Moynihan's book argues that the antipoverty program produced "maximum feasible misunderstanding" in contrast to his 1965 view that the Economic Opportunity Act represented far the best example of "the professionalization of reform." By 1969, Moynihan had come to the conclusion that, "the government did not know what it was doing."[9] This was "the essential fact" in the whole community action effort. Moynihan is fearful that young people in the future, looking back to the 1960s, will see "the debacle;" to their understanding, the community action program will appear a "sell-out." He closes his book lamenting "the soaring rhetoric, the minimum of performance; the feigned controversy, the private betrayal; in the end . . . the sell-out."[10] The words are those of a professional who had something to dó with both rhetoric and performance in the Kennedy, Johnson, and Nixon administrations.

Since Moynihan joined the Nixon administration after writing this gloomy evaluation, it is fair to assume that he saw another aspect of the situation. Curiously enough, in the same book, *Maximum Feasible Misunderstanding,* he also quotes from an OEO-sponsored study of nine community action programs showing a number of positive results for those individuals who were reached by the program. The excerpt from the study conducted by Daniel Yankelovich, Inc. is reproduced below exactly as it appears in Moynihan's book:

> The large majority of the poor reached by CAA programs report significant changes in their own and their children's lives as a result of their participation. For their children, they report improvements both in school and at home. For themselves, they report a mix of tangible and intangible benefits including new jobs, special training, more earnings, education, stretching available dollars further, improvement of neighborhoods, and increased hope, self-respect, and confidence in the future (mixed with an intense impatience especially on the part of the Negro

families to share in the affluence they see in the rest of the society).[11]

This hardly suggests a sell-out. Was it, perhaps, a mirage? Moynihan felt that "a measure of reality testing" might be in order. He wondered whether the improvements noted were observable to others besides those who reported them, a singular query from a critic who usually questions the role of middle-class professionals as spokesmen for the poor. In any event, Moynihan thought the survey indicated that "the community action agencies can produce results even if such do not always add up to a social revolution."[12] The dilemma persists: individuals say they are helped, but the results fall short of fundamental social reform.

As I have written elsewhere, ". . . one is not always sure whether Moynihan regards community action as a great mistake or as an important and necessary social innovation. We should not be as harsh on Moynihan on this score as some have been, because no one can be completely sure what the full significance of community action may have been. Perhaps, as in nuclear physics, we shall discover one day in our study of politics that basic elements may be contradictory and yet have validity."[13]

COMMUNITY ACTION AND SOCIAL REFORM

Moynihan is also one of the few observers among the eminent critics of the program to note the role played by Jack Conway and a small group of associates in trying to mould community action as an instrument of basic social reform. During the first year of operation, Conway served as Shriver's principal deputy in charge of community action. Conway subsequently told Richard Blumenthal, a Moynihan protégé, that "his concern was to structure community action programs so that they would have an immediate and irreversible impact on the communities."[14]

Moynihan described Conway as follows:

> An immensely competent man . . . Conway had no particular intention of making trouble for the Johnson administration, but his first concern was in another direction. Where the President wished to help the poor, *Conway wished to arouse them.* That, in

a sense, was his profession. He was a labor organizer on the militant wing of the labor movement.[15]

Conway was on loan to OEO from his position as head of the Industrial Unions Department of the national AFL-CIO. Knowledgeable Washington observers thought of Jack Conway as Walter Reuther's principal representative in the nation's capital. Conway's willingness to serve as the chief administrator of community action during the program's formative year suggests that some people involved in the program knew what they were doing—or trying to do. Moynihan nevertheless reports that "the Conway group gave to the community action programs of the poverty program a structure that neither those who drafted it, those who sponsored it, nor those who enacted it ever in any way intended. . . ."[16] The analysis in this book does not support Moynihan's interpretation. There were people involved in the drafting and sponsoring of the act who became important members of the Conway group, Richard Boone being a notable example. The point should perhaps be revised to say that Moynihan and certain other members of the Shriver task force did not anticipate clearly what the Conway group attempted. Retrospective statements by Yarmolinsky, Moynihan, and Sundquist—key members of the Shriver task force—suggest that some of the leading technicians who had a hand in drawing up the act proved to be rather poor judges of the program's political potential, thus confirming a major thesis of this book.

On the central issue of the meaning of "maximum feasible participation," Yarmolinsky later reported that he had understood the phrase to mean simply that services should be "carried out by poor people who lived in the area." "The concept of promoting control of the program by the poor did not surface during this early period of discussion."[17] Yarmolinsky has also been quoted as saying that the objectives of the drafters was never to "get the poor to think of themselves as a political force. This didn't occur to us and it didn't occur to any of the highly professional politicians we consulted."[18] Moynihan's perception was that if the poor and especially the Blacks *in the South* were "not sharing—that is, participating—in the benfits of the new program, Washington could intervene on the grounds that the requirements of the legislation were not being met."[19] Sundquist later recalled: "Nobody listened much. If you have a program for somebody, you want him to participate, you want the maximum number of people to be affected. It seemed very obvious, very innocuous."[20]

Perhaps they should have listened more carefully. The concept seemed obvious only to those members of the technical elite who assumed that the tame version of "self-help" would prevail. The social and political potential of maximum feasible participation was quite different if the perceived objective was fundamental social reform. Moynihan, Yarmolinsky, and Sundquist were among those who missed the potential meaning which the concept might have in poverty neighborhoods because they opted for a more conventional approach.[21] It is most unlikely that Jack Conway and Richard Boone read the phrase in the narrow sense of preventing segregation in Southern antipoverty programs. There were inevitable risks in Conway's approach, not the least being the near certainty of provoking a defensive reaction on the part of established local authorities. The risk was evidently judged worth taking if the program were to move beyond the providing of social services to the poor through traditional channels. Conway, experienced in the Washington policy struggle and aware that community action was living on borrowed time, chose the more provocative version.

GOVERNMENT CHALLENGES THE ESTABLISHED ORDER

Kenneth Clark's criticism recognizes the inherent difficulty in community action once it is seen as an instrument for fundamental social reform.

The paradox of the community action programs is this: the programs need, and have received, support from government, i.e. the established order; yet their very effectiveness depends on challenging the same order and transforming society itself.[22]

A national program which uses federal funds in challenging the established order and in transforming society ranks among the most interesting of contemporary social experiments. The success or failure of such a program is hardly a trivial matter. At the same time, Clark sees the terribly limited aspect of the program so long as it functions as simply another form of self-help. When the victims of long-standing social injustice are expected to change injustice on their own, the situation is comparable to asking the sick person to get himself well, Clark observes. He has no doubt about the outcome under these circumstances. His early review of community action projects in twelve major cities convinced him that rhetorical flourishes were likely to outweigh the potential for social reform. The program, as he found it, leaned heavily on the traditional approach, providing social services to people in need while placing relatively little emphasis on poor people taking social action to right the injustices which dominate their lives. On reflection the programs seemed to Clark "a charade, an exhilarating intellectual game whose players never understood the nature of power and the reluctance of those who have it to share it."[23] The greatest defect, in his view, was that the poor people themselves were not taken seriously. Clark has an explicit standard to apply: a key sign of the effectiveness of an antipoverty program is "observable evidence of social change, not only the modifying of poverty itself, but of the psychological context of poverty."[24]

Seen from the vantage point of the early 1970s, it is obvious that the antipoverty program of the 1960s did not constitute a real "war" against poverty. The major battles in such a war were never fought. Throughout its history, the antipoverty program has been limited in every important respect: narrow in scope, conceptually ambiguous, inadequately funded, and lacking in sustained support in the White House, in the Congress, and among the general public. Community action, as Moynihan and Blumenthal have shown, was plagued from the outset by widely divergent notions about its purposes. Well-intentioned technicians in the old Bureau of the Budget thought they saw a means of coordinating a number of federal activities in local communities and neighborhoods. Equally well-intentioned men who were responsible at the national level for the central administration of community action during the first crucial years saw in it a potential instrument of social action, a means of encouraging poor people in the arts and skills of politics and organization. The available evidence supports Clark's assessment that this latter approach proved largely abortive:

> The actual programs operated under the heading of community action programs were for the most part traditional social services, opportunity or educational programs and did not directly provide the poor with the opportunity or the skill to obtain and

exercise the power required to bring about observable changes in their living conditions.[25]

Thus, Howard Hallman's study, prepared in 1967 for Senator Joseph Clark's Senate Committee on Manpower, examined thirty-five poverty agencies and found no instance of an indigenous group of the poor having initiated a program, although civil rights groups had done so in eight cases.[26]

A more recent appraisal by John H. Strange found that "only a few (one or two percent) of the community action programs were ever substantially controlled by or influenced by the poor or by ethnic minorities."[27] In this vital respect, community action was far from effecting a major social transformation.

To conclude that the community action effort, overall, fell short of effecting a social revolution is not necessarily to conclude that the experience has had no positive impact. One of the most impressive examinations of community action at the local level, prepared by Ralph M. Kramer, suggests a more complex situation. Kramer, who undertook a comparative analysis of several community action programs in the San Francisco Bay area during the first three years of the program, found that:

> Residents of the target areas, including a very small proportion of low-income persons, demonstrated their ability to serve in policy-making, advisory, program planning, review, administrative and budgeting roles. At the outcome of federal intervention, a significant precedent was set for community decision-making in that the definition of who should be included in that community was broadened. In the often confused and contentious efforts to develop and conduct programs with the participation of the residents of target areas, numerous economic and political benefits accrued principally to various members of minority groups.[28]

At the same time, Kramer noted that resident participation all too easily became an end in itself, a kind of "numbers game:"

> As a result, much of what took place in the name of maximum feasible participation during the first three years had little to do with the reduction of poverty or changing institutions but could best be justified on socio-therapeutic grounds.[29]

OEO'S POSITIVE ROLE

However, OEO's Community Affairs Office was successful in devising and initiating at least three national programs which have provided important new services for the poor. Legal Services and Upward Bound enjoyed broad support in the Congress throughout the first four years of the Nixon administration, despite their origins in the Johnson era. By 1972, a congressional majority was ready to transform Head Start into an enlarged and expanded program for child care and development, even in the face of a presidential veto. Given the desire to do so on the part of the dominant political leadership in the nation, each of these programs, and the Neighborhood Youth Corps as well, could readily be expanded; each could, within a matter of months, be shaped and enriched so as to increase its program effectiveness. There was no technical limitation stipulating that Head Start, for example, should enroll only one child in every five or ten who might benefit.

Criticism of the antipoverty program is also likely to obscure the sharp decline in the incidence of poverty which occurred between 1959 and 1969. Actually, there were 14 million fewer Americans below the official poverty line in 1969 than in 1959. Table 4 shows the incidence of poverty and its distribution, state by state, in the 1960s, thus revealing the improvement which took place. While there is no reason to assume that the antipoverty program was a prime factor in producing this, the change itself is significant. The avowedly expansionist budgetary and fiscal policies of the Kennedy-Johnson administrations had a favorable impact on employment. The unemployment rate when President Kennedy took office approached 7 percent, a sickeningly high level. Before President Johnson left the White House, unemployment had been cut in half. The 3.5 percent rate which Johnson bequeathed his successor stood well below the interim goal of 4 percent set by Walter Heller's Council of Economic Advisers in the early Kennedy years. Unfortunately, the decline in the unemployment rate to between 5 and 3.5 percent occurred after the economy had been subjected to the heavy additional expenditures attributed to Vietnam. Vietnam spending approximated one hundred billion dollars during the Johnson era. As a result, defense-related employment increased by almost two million between fiscal years 1964 and 1968. Then as

TABLE 4

Distribution and Incidence of Poverty, 1959–1969

State	Thousands of Poor Persons*		Percentage Distribution		Poverty Incidence (%)	
	1959	1969**	1959	1969*	1959	1969*
UNITED STATES	38,681	24,289	100.0	100.0	22.1	12.2
Alabama	1,374	787	3.6	3.2	42.5	22.6
Alaska	38	35	.1	.1	19.0	12.6
Arizona	314	212	.8	.9	24.9	12.7
Arkansas	843	433	2.2	1.8	48.3	22.0
California	2,199	1,879	5.7	7.1	14.4	9.0
Colorado	312	269	.8	1.1	18.3	13.0
Connecticut	236	163	.6	.7	9.6	5.5
Delaware	73	94	.2	.4	16.8	17.7
District of Columbia	161	120	.4	.5	22.2	15.2
Florida	1,371	1,172	3.5	4.8	28.4	18.7
Georgia	1,505	837	3.9	3.4	39.0	18.3
Hawaii	102	49	.3	.2	17.1	6.3
Idaho	124	56	.3	.2	18.7	7.9
Illinois	1,446	932	3.7	3.8	14.7	8.6
Indiana	797	572	2.1	2.4	17.5	11.3
Iowa	583	328	1.5	1.4	21.5	12.0
Kansas	418	248	1.1	1.0	19.7	10.8
Kentucky	1,137	411	2.9	1.7	38.3	12.9
Louisiana	1,274	852	3.3	3.5	39.5	23.1
Maine	222	133	.6	.5	23.7	13.8
Maryland	523	431	1.4	1.8	17.4	11.6
Massachusetts	608	352	1.6	1.4	12.2	6.5
Michigan	1,216	827	3.1	3.4	15.9	9.6
Minnesota	646	319	1.7	1.3	19.3	8.7
Mississippi	1,173	738	3.0	3.0	54.5	31.7
Missouri	1,051	870	2.7	3.6	24.9	19.0
Montana	129	86	.3	.4	19.5	12.6
Nebraska	309	196	.8	.8	22.3	13.7
Nevada	35	37	.1	.2	12.8	8.2
New Hampshire	87	65	.2	.3	14.9	9.2
New Jersey	673	434	1.7	1.8	11.3	6.2
New Mexico	278	167	.7	.7	29.9	17.0
New York	2,319	1,513	6.0	6.2	14.2	8.4
North Carolina	1,796	744	4.6	3.1	40.6	14.6
North Dakota	169	65	.4	.3	27.1	10.7
Ohio	1,508	1,111	3.9	4.6	15.9	10.5
Oklahoma	680	430	1.8	1.8	29.9	17.0
Oregon	262	190	.7	.8	15.1	9.5
Pennsylvania	1,881	1,286	4.9	5.3	12.0	11.1
Rhode Island	135	91	.4	.4	16.5	10.1
South Carolina	1,049	422	2.7	1.7	45.4	15.9
South Dakota	202	77	.5	.3	30.1	11.8
Tennessee	1,374	652	3.6	2.7	39.3	16.6
Texas	2,970	2,030	7.7	8.4	31.7	18.4
Utah	135	90	.4	.4	15.4	8.7
Vermont	88	52	.2	.2	23.5	12.0
Virginia	1,164	704	3.0	2.9	30.6	15.3
Washington	397	260	1.0	1.1	14.3	7.8
West Virginia	637	301	1.6	1.2	34.6	16.8
Wisconsin	607	277	1.6	1.1	15.7	6.6
Wyoming	51	34	.1	.1	15.6	10.8

*Definition of the poor is derived from a formula based on income, size of family, place of residence. (Weekly Report p. 703)
**Preliminary figures

SOURCE: Office of Planning, Research and Evaluation, Office of Economic Opportunity
Copyright 1970 by The Congressional Quarterly, Inc. Reprinted by permission.

defense spending declined after 1968, largely due to the reduced American military effort in Vietnam, defense-related employment fell from 7.8 million in 1968 to 5.9 million in 1971.[30]

The experience of the Kennedy-Johnson years indicates that it is easier to get support for a high level of public expenditure when matters of national security are involved than for domestic programs, but it would be a mistake to assume that the American venture in Vietnam was "planned" within the institutionalized presidency as a means of easing domestic employment problems. The favorable impact on domestic employment was more an ironic than premeditated byproduct of military escalation in Vietnam during the 1960s.

"Selected Unemployment Rates" and "Unemployment by Race" for years 1961–1971 (tables 5 and 6) reveal the dramatic improve-

TABLE 5

SELECTED UNEMPLOYMENT RATES 1961–1971

(Percent of Labor Force Categories)

	1961	1962	1963	1964	1965	1966	1967	1968	1969	1970	1971
All Civilian Workers	6.7	5.5	5.7	5.2	4.5	3.8	3.8	3.6	3.5	4.9	5.9
All Male Workers	6.4	5.2	5.2	4.6	4.0	3.2	3.1	2.9	2.8	4.4	5.3
All Female Workers	7.2	6.2	6.5	6.2	5.5	4.8	5.2	4.8	4.7	5.9	6.9
Men (over age 20)	5.7	4.6	4.5	3.9	3.2	2.5	2.3	2.2	2.1	3.5	4.4
Women (over age 20)	6.3	5.4	5.4	5.2	4.5	3.8	4.2	3.8	3.7	4.8	5.7
Married Men	4.6	3.6	3.4	2.8	2.4	1.9	1.8	1.6	1.5	2.6	3.2
Married Women	6.5	5.4	5.4	5.1	4.5	3.7	4.5	3.9	3.9	4.9	5.7
All Over Age 55	5.3	4.3	4.1	3.7	3.2	2.6	2.5	2.2	2.0	2.8	3.4
Insured Workers*	5.6	4.4	4.3	3.8	3.0	2.3	2.5	2.2	2.1	3.4	4.1

Insured unemployed as percent of all insured workers.

SOURCE: U.S. Labor Department

TABLE 6

UNEMPLOYMENT BY RACE 1961–1971

(Percent of Labor Force Categories)

	1961	1962	1963	1964	1965	1966	1967	1968	1969	1970	1971
All Civilian Workers	6.7	5.5	5.7	5.2	4.5	3.8	3.8	3.6	3.5	4.9	5.9
White Adult	5.3	4.2	4.2	3.8	3.3	2.6	2.7	2.5	2.4	3.7	4.5
Minority Adult*	11.2	9.8	9.3	8.2	6.6	5.6	5.5	5.0	4.6	6.2	7.9
White Men	5.1	4.0	3.9	3.4	2.9	2.2	2.1	2.0	1.9	3.2	4.0
Minority Men*	11.7	10.0	9.2	7.7	6.0	4.9	4.3	3.9	3.7	5.6	7.2
White Women	5.7	4.7	4.8	4.6	4.0	3.3	3.8	3.4	3.4	4.4	5.3
Minority Women*	10.6	9.6	9.4	9.0	7.5	6.6	7.1	6.3	5.8	6.9	8.7

Black and other minority races.

SOURCE: U.S. Labor Department

ment in employment during the prime years of military escalation as well as the rapid rise in unemployment which took place in 1970–71.[31]

The official figures showed 24.3 million Americans below the poverty line in 1969.[32] After a long period of decline, the number of people living in poverty increased sharply as the Nixon administration unfolded disinflationary policies aimed at slowing down the annual rate of growth. There were 25.5 million Americans living in poverty in 1970, an increase of 1.2 million in one year.[33] There was a slight increase to 25.6 million in 1971; this was deemed "statistically insignificant" since the increase fell well within the sampling error of 356,000. More than 15 million people were receiving federally-aided public assistance (i.e. public welfare) in March, 1972. Children and their mothers totaled 10.9 million while the blind, the crippled, and the indigent aged accounted for the rest.[34] As the figures in table 6 show, non-white Americans suffer disproportionately when disinflationary policies are pursued. The "for whites only" aspect of the official full employment doctrine discussed on pages 99–103 of Chapter 7 turns nightmarish for poor blacks when the full employment objective is put aside in favor of a policy which accepts an average unemployment rate of 5.5 to 6 percent, as during the Nixon years. Although a policy of economic growth taken by itself will not eliminate poverty in the United States, the experience in the 1950s, partially repeated in the early 1970s, suggests that an official preoccupation with economic restraint will inevitably exacerbate the plight of the poor while increasing their numbers.[35]

The antipoverty program, taken as a whole, also tends to be undervalued for the organizational contribution it has often made in poverty areas. It would be difficult to find an urban poverty neighborhood in the early 1970s which did not have in it one or more organizations funded with monies at least partially derived from the Economic Opportunity Act. Many of these local organizations did not exist prior to 1964. These organizations have provided political and organizational experience not only to professionals but to sizeable numbers of indigenous workers and, though this has occurred less frequently, to the neighborhood poor themselves. Kenneth Clark and others have minimized this aspect of the program, passing over rather lightly, it would seem, the upward mobility effect antipoverty programs have had on the career patterns of many of these people. While Clark was doubtless correct in sensing the danger that some indigenous workers in the neighborhoods might have signed on in order to enjoy the economic rewards of a new kind of "hustling," other factors, including the desire to serve, were at work in many local communities. Furthermore, the Neighborhood Youth Corps, often criticized for not being a technically sophisticated operation in many local situations, has provided public service job experience for several hundred thousand young people each year. In less than a decade, the NYC has placed more than two billion dollars in the hands of literally millions of young people who needed the money.[36] Thus, the Neighborhood Youth Corps enrolled 756,100 youths in calendar year 1971; 49,600 in the out-of-school program, 97,200 in the in-school program, and 609,300 in the summer jobs program. The cost of the summer program was $257.9 million in 1971. The same program was alloted $377.6 million, a record high, to provide nine weeks' employment for 740,222 young people in the summer of 1972. More than 70 percent of the 1971 summer program enrollees were from minority groups.[37]

Kenneth Clark is certainly not wrong in asserting that the Johnson administration failed to take the poor people seriously. At the same time, the poor people in responding to the opportunities put forward in the more reformist version of community action often took themselves seriously. There is a direct linkage in more than a few communities between the demand for "community control," usually involving schools, and an earlier experience with community action programs. Alan A. Altshuler, who has examined the black demand for participation in the larger cities, concludes: "The whole current movement for neighborhood control was largely set in motion by the 'maximum feasible participation' provision of the Economic Opportunity Act of 1964."[38] The demand for neighborhood control and the broader urge for participation in the governance of communities is likely to intensify rather than to diminish in the 1970s.

In some cases experience in local antipoverty programs has led to direct participation in electoral politics, thus feeding into a broader secular trend in which new black leaders are elected mayors of important cities and as representatives in state legislatures and in the national House of Representatives. Howard Hallman, who has probably examined closely more local community action projects than any other qualified observer, has written:

> Another factor is the use of the new organizations by community leaders to build a power base which is transferable to other arenas. Members of Congress saw this for the first time in 1966 when in some Congressional districts persons identified with the Community Action Program (mostly lay leaders but sometimes staff) began to turn up in the ranks of their opposition in primaries and the general election. As if to confirm their suspicions, two out of the 12 black members now in Congress (Parren Mitchell and Ronald Dellums) advanced in their communities through involvement in the Community Action Program. The delegate to Congress from the District of Columbia (Walter Fauntroy) was the head of a neighborhood renewal organization supported by federal urban renewal funds. And the current president of the Navajo Tribal Council, Peter McDonald, was previously executive director of the tribal community action agency. Other less notable examples are plentiful around the country. While their political activities have been legally separate, they have demonstrated their leadership abilities through citizen organizations and developed a following in their communities.[39]

There is a direct relationship between the expansion of the welfare universe, the emergence of welfare rights as a national issue, and the antipoverty program, as Frances Fox Piven and Richard A. Cloward have shown.[40] Noting that some 800,000 families were added to welfare rolls, an increase of 107 percent, between December, 1960, and February, 1969, Piven and Cloward suggest that the explosive increase is directly linked to a new welfare-rights awareness among the poor which in turn is related to a new kind of welfare-rights service that became prevalent in the 1960s. The new service was based, typically, in the so-called "storefront service center" located in a slum neighborhood. Most of the centers, perhaps a thousand in all, were sponsored by community action agencies. Piven and Cloward also note the effectiveness of the legal assault on welfare restrictions, a process which "originated mainly with OEO's neighborhood legal services program."[41] The welfare explosion continued into the 1970s. The main stimulus for the upsurge in numbers after 1969, Piven and Cloward insist, was the

Nixon administration's anti-inflation strategy which doubled the number of unemployed in a brief period of time.

WAS IT FOR REAL?

Young people in the 1970s may be curious about the early days of the antipoverty program. They are likely to ask, "Was it for real?" It will be remarkable if many of them do not anticipate a cynical response in view of the principal critiques available to them. This book aspires to present an analysis which is as complex as the reality it tries to deal with. It, therefore, needs to be emphasized, since other accounts have neglected it, that the prevailing spirit of the people in OEO who worked on the program in 1964 and 1965 was not cynical-manipulative. Even when the other side of the Johnson White House had begun the process of military escalation in Vietnam, a process which was soon to have a devastating effect on the "war" against poverty, the dominant spirit in OEO headquarters was one of generous enthusiasm and decent commitment to making the program as effective as possible. It has been argued in more recent years, with all of the benefit of hindsight, that while domestic programs proliferated in the 1960s, there was no "policy."[42] There is obvious merit in having clear and intelligent "overall" policy, just as there is value in having operational programs which are addressed to real and specific human needs. Our analysis has shown, however, that while the policy objective—to wage unconditional war against poverty—was declared in the 1964 state-of-the-union message, there was no lasting national commitment to the objective. The President backed away from his own program while pursuing an obsessive and elusive goal in Southeast Asia; the Congress never focused clearly on the issue; and the general public remained either supremely indifferent or mildly hostile.

President Johnson has this distinct recollection:

> I told Douglass Cater of the *Reporter* magazine—who later came to work for me at the White House—that I did not know whether we would pass a single law or appropriate a single dollar. But one thing I did know: When I got through, no one in the country would be able to ignore the poverty in our midst.[43]

It depends, no doubt, on the vantage point. Mr. Johnson is gone from office, and millions of his fellow countrymen apparently have managed not to let "the poverty in their midst" concern them unduly. The Economic Opportunity Act survived into the early 1970s largely because its programs had grown familiar as part of the ongoing process; most of them were viewed in the congressional arena as portions of the manpower-structural-employment policy "revolution" of the 1960s. The general perception of these programs at the level of the attentive public had little to do with the eradication of poverty per se. The whole experience raises once again the perennial question: how is fundamental social and economic reform to be effected in a national political system which resists the creation of a solid political majority in favor of *anything?* Professionalization of reform is likely to produce modest results, at best, unless the plans and programs which the professionals devise enjoy the sustained support of a determinedly reformist political leadership located in the center of the system. The leadership in the struggle must come from the White House, and the struggle must be engaged because the forces and institutions opposed to fundamental reform are powerful and deeply entrenched.[44]

The Economic Opportunity Act produced a cluster of programs with a potential for getting at some of the basic aspects of poverty in this country. Writing in 1967, Marris and Rein identified a number of purposes which were given new expression in the antipoverty program:

> . . . executive social planning; the marshalling of protest against exploitation and neglect; advocacy and advice; applied research into the techniques of service and the structure of social welfare; the creation of jobs and new forms of training; the reinterpretation of the language of schooling, so that it makes some sense to the children of the ghettos; the rebuilding of the ghettos themselves. . . .[45]

If the list of purposes seems today an overly-generous one, it is also relevant to the experience of the 1960s that two such sophisticated social observers perceived so much potential in the program. At the same time, Marris and Rein understood the largest obstacle to the fulfillment of these entirely sensible purposes:

> Yet in itself, none of these innovations, however imaginative, can achieve much without the funds which only a national re-

allocation of resources could provide. Their progress depends on the amount of money which the nation as a whole is willing to devote to them. If America is inhibited by its political philosophy from drawing up a master plan for the Great Society, it needs all the more an overmastering commitment to the ideals community action represents.[46]

No such overmastering commitment to these ideals was made. The nation escalated the war in Southeast Asia in the 1960s while de-escalating the "war" against poverty at home. The single most important fact about the programs authorized by the Economic Opportunity Act is that they were never funded at a level adequate to meet the universe of need to which they were directed. The entire antipoverty effort from fiscal years 1965 to 1973 cost approximately $15.5 billion. Expenditures for the war in Vietnam during the same period totalled some $120 billion. As Sargent Shriver testified in 1966, in the midst of military escalation, a war fought with half the bullets is not going to be effective; the war against poverty received significantly less than half the bullets needed.[47]

This analysis has resisted the notion that the government did not know what it was doing in launching the war on poverty, while emphasizing the lack of commitment to basic social reform. There were conflicting notions about community action. There is reason to question whether President Johnson clearly understood the meaning of his own program as it related to the anguished cry from the dark ghettos. Still it is irresponsible to suggest that there was not a serious and conscientious purpose behind the program in its formative years, especially among the people who directed the OEO programs at the national level. There are difficulties enough to be encountered in making an accurate assessment of the Economic Opportunity Act without accepting this distortion of reality. The Economic Opportunity Act, plagued by limited funds, resisted by all of those forces in American society which always impede social reform, given certain limited tools as well as an important presidential boost at the outset, represented an unprecedented effort to get at several aspects of poverty. It was a partial program and it soon suffered from presidential neglect, but the people responsible for administering OEO during the vital early years were not cynics manipulating the poor in order to stifle an incipient revolution of the proletariat.[48]

A CLEAR WARNING

We have been examining the nation's experience with an anti-poverty program in the decade of the 1960s. It may very well be fitting, a decade hence, in assessing the politics of the 1970s, to seek the connections between the "Community Action-maximum feasible participation" struggles of the 1960s and the neo-populist strain which became so clearly visible in the presidential election of 1972.[49] The devotees of the new politics in the 1970s seemed destined to confront certain aspects of the dilemma which thwarted the antipoverty program. The urge to decentralize and to encourage popular participation in decision making is powerfully felt in the modern technocratic society, but "the forces that maintain deprivation and alienation—among them institutional racism, low income, unavailability of jobs and underemployment—are largely beyond the pale of neighborhood action."[50] It seems most unlikely that very many of the basic social and economic problems plaguing American society in the 1970s will be solved from a neighborhood base. Set against this side of reality is the demand in the black community for community control stemming from a desire "to restructure decision-making institutions in urban areas in order to maximize the ability of local residents to govern."[51] The psychological imperative behind this demand is clear enough. The experience with the community action program, however, carries a warning which is equally clear:

> The community development process is no substitute for that massive commitment of national resources required to eliminate poverty by rebuilding the ghetto and restoring full citizenship to minorities, although it may be able to mobilize support for these social policies.[52]

A study of the politics of poverty has much to teach us about the poverty of politics in the recent past.[53]

NOTES

CHAPTER 1

[1]Tom Wicker, *New York Times,* January 9, 1964.

[2]Rowland Evans and Robert Novak, *Lyndon B. Johnson: The Exercise of Power* (New York, 1966), pp. 5-17, Lyndon Johnson, running in a special congressional election in 1937, publicly supported President Roosevelt on the "Court-packing" issue, and, hence, attracted the attention of the President. FDR later encouraged men like Harry Hopkins and Harold Ickes to open a good many doors for the freshman congressman from West Texas.

[3]Arthur Meier Schlesinger, Jr., *A Thousand Days* (Boston, 1965), p. 708.

[4]Richard Neustadt, *Presidential Power* (New York, 1960), pp. 58-59.

[5]Schlesinger, p. 1011. John Bibby and Roger Davidson, in their book *On Capitol Hill* (New York, 1967), pinpoint the date of the Heller-Kennedy conversation as November 19, 1963. They write: "Before departing with the Cabinet for a trip to Japan, Heller obtained a hurried interview with President Kennedy. He asked whether work should go forward under the assumption that an antipoverty measure would be included in the 1964 legislative agenda. Kennedy's answer was immediate: 'Yes, and let me see your proposals in a couple of weeks' " (p. 226).

Bibby and Davidson's Chapter 7, in which this appears, is an excellent brief analysis of the forces which came together in making the Economic Opportunity Act. Unfortunately, their work is marred by an astonishing casualness about sources. In the paragraph quoted above, for example, no source is given for the conversation between the chairman of the Council of Economic Advisers and the President. Yet, the authors feel free to quote the President directly.

[6]Bibby and Davidson's Chapter 6, "The Power of the Rules—The Tangled History of the Depressed Areas Act," is a tightly written, brief history of ARA which emphasizes the role of procedures in congressional politics.

CHAPTER 2

[1]See Charles Silberman, *Crisis in Black and White* (New York, 1964), for more detail on the Ford Foundation gray areas program. Silberman is critical of Ylvisaker's approach and, in fact, defends Saul Alinsky's direct action methods.

[2]A great deal has been made at one time or another about the contribution of Michael Harrington to the war on poverty. There can be no doubt that Harrington's brilliant book, *The Other America* (New York, 1962), touched the national conscience. We are told that President Kennedy read Harrington's book. We know that Harrington is one of the "experts" Shriver called to Washington. Harrington is both an attractive and energetic evangelist for social reform, but the precise nature of his influence on any program idea in the Economic Opportunity Act has not been identified.

[3]See Brian Smith, "The Role of the Poor in the Poverty Program: the Origin and Development of Maximum Feasible Participation" (unpublished Master's thesis, Department of Public Law and Government, Columbia University, 1966). Smith convincingly shows that community action and "participation of the poor" came directly from the juvenile delinquency

committee staff. Smith, who interviewed several key government officials, identifies Richard Boone of the committee staff as the person who was most directly responsible. I am convinced on the basis of my own research and many informal conversations with knowledgeable individuals, including members of the Shriver task force, that this is an accurate assessment.

[4]Bibby and Davidson, p. 236.

[5]*Hearings Before the Subcommittee on the War on Poverty Program: The Economic Opportunity Act of 1964,* Part 1, 1964, p. 305.

[6]Daniel P. Moynihan has reported that community action as a concept was not changed at all from the first task force draft through the enactment of the bill in final form. See his article "What is Community Action?" *(The Public Interest,* Vol. 5, Fall, 1966), pp. 3–8.

[7]Evans and Novak, *Lyndon B. Johnson,* pp. 432–33.

[8]Bibby and Davidson, p. 238.

[9]*Ibid.,* pp. 249–50.

CHAPTER 3

[1]Herbert Krosney, *Beyond Welfare: Poverty in the Supercity* (New York, 1966), p. 8.

[2]Nathan Glazer and Daniel Patrick Moynihan, *Beyond the Melting Pot* (Cambridge, Mass., 1963), pp. 120–21.

[3]See Krosney for an analysis of various interpretations of "maximum feasible participation" which grew out of earlier experience in the Mobilization for Youth project in New York City, a project which had the support and interest of the Ford Foundation, the President's Committee on Juvenile Delinquency, and, at a later stage, HEW and the Labor Department.

[4]Quoted in Krosney, p. 16.

CHAPTER 4

[1]See *Intergovernmental Relations in the Poverty Program,* a report of the Advisory Commission on Intergovernmental Relations (April, 1966). The commission report, which draws upon research done by Sar A. Levitan for a forthcoming study by the W. E. Upjohn Institute for Employment Research, states (p. 21): "Sensitive to the need for arousing widespread public interest and support, Shriver reacted negatively to the idea of a limited program of scattered demonstration activities."

[2]See Mr. Shriver's statement in *Hearings Before the Subcommittee on the War on Poverty Program of the Committee on Education and Labor: 1966 Amendments to the Economic Opportunity Act of 1964,* March 8, 1966.

[3]This section is based largely on an excellent article by Barbara Carter, "Sargent Shriver and the Role of the Poor," which appeared in *The Reporter,* May 5, 1966. Miss Carter's assessment of this phase of community action is corroborated by the daily reporting of Joseph Loftus of the *New York Times* and Eve Edstrom of the *Washington Post,* both of whom have followed with great skill and thoroughness the many vacillations in OEO policy and practices. I have also relied heavily on their reports.

[4]The meeting between Mayor Daley's committee and the Vice-President is reported in Jules Witcover and Erwain Knoll, "Politics and the Poor: Shriver's Second Thoughts," *The Reporter,* December 30, 1965. I have relied on this article in this section, and have found that it re-enforces reports filed frequently throughout this period by Joseph Loftus in the *New York Times* and Eve Edstrom in the *Washington Post.*

[5]See Charles E. Silberman, *Crisis in Black and White,* for a friendly and admiring view of Alinsky, his philosophy, tactics, and accomplishments, especially Chapter 10, "The Revolt Against 'Welfare Colonialism,'" an account of Alinsky's influence on the Woodlawn Organization in Chicago. TWO (as it is often called) is an organization in the Chicago Negro ghetto which has struggled with some effectiveness against the University of Chicago and Mayor Richard Daley.

[6]Elmer Eric Schattschneider, *The Semisovereign People* (New York, 1960), pp. 98-99.

CHAPTER 5

[1]See report by Alfred Friendly, *Washington Post,* February 1, 1966.

[2]Rowland Evans and Robert Novak, *Washington Post,* January 14, 1966.

[3]See article by Wallace Turner, "Congress Critical of Shriver Office, Curbs Poverty Programs," *New York Times,* November 2, 1965.

[4]All of the quotations are taken from the *Hearings Before the Subcommittee on the War on Poverty Program of the Committee on Education and Labor,* Part 1, 1966.

[5]*New York Times,* April 12, 1966.

[6]As reported by Eve Edstrom in the *Washington Post,* April 14, 1966.

[7]Nan Robertson, *New York Times,* April 15, 1966.

[8]*Ibid.*

[9]Associated Press, April 15, 1966.

[10]Eve Edstrom, *Washington Post,* April 19, 1966; see also *New York Times,* same day.

[11]See Mark R. Arnold, "Behind a Demonstration: Some Planning, Much Anger," *The National Observer,* May 9, 1966. This may well be the most complete account thus far of this strange episode. Arnold was able to find no evidence of an advance plot to disrupt the meeting. He writes: "Rather the demonstration erupted as a consequence of the impatience and frustration of some of the impoverished at the meeting over the pace of antipoverty measures and over the direction of the conference itself." In a real sense, the outburst which the Shriver address provoked was also a reaction among "militant" slum organizers against the Crusade's leadership as much as it was a protest against Shriver's bland optimism.

[12]As reported by Joseph A. Loftus, *New York Times,* April 28, 1966.

[13]Eve Edstrom, *Washington Post,* May 16, 1966.

[14]*New York Times,* April 20, 1966.

[15]*Congressional Quarterly Weekly Report,* XXIV, No. 38 (Sept. 23, 1966).

[16]*U.S. Congressional Record,* 89th Cong. 2d Sess., 1966, CXI, p. 22813.

[17]*Ibid.,* p. 24122.

CHAPTER 6

[1]See Barbara Carter, "The Great Society: A Man with a Problem," *The Reporter,* May 20, 1965, for a brief view of Dr. Deutsch, his work, and his apprehensions about Head Start as a crash program.

[2]Facts and figures on the development of Head Start are derived from an account appearing in *Congressional Quarterly Weekly Report,* March 18, 1966, p. 626.

[3]Wallace Turner, *New York Times,* November 2, 1965.

[4]*Ibid.*

[5]*Congressional Quarterly Weekly Reports,* March 18, 1966, p. 616.

[6]William C. Selover, *Christian Science Monitor,* October 19, 1966.

[7]*Ibid.*

[8]For detailed accounts see *ibid.* and Roy Reed in the *New York Times,* October 23, 1966.

[9]*New York Times,* October 23, 1966.

[10]*Christian Science Monitor,* October 19, 1966.

[11]*Ibid.* The reporter was William C. Selover.

[12]Jean R. Hailey, *Washington Post,* October 25, 1966.

[13]See *Congressional Quarterly Weekly Report,* November 11, 1966, p. 2804: "Based on a key 1965 roll call vote, the old House was 240 in favor, 191 opposed. The program has lost 49 supporters and now faces a House breakdown of 225 opposed, 191 in favor and 19 undecided." Joseph A. Loftus came to a similar conclusion using a different key vote: "A vote in the House on September 29 tested the program's standing. The motion called for striking the enacting clause—killing the bill. The motion failed 208 to 156. If 45 of the 208 switched to the other side, the bill would be killed, 201 to 163." *New York Times,* November 13, 1966.

[14]Eve Edstrom, *Washington Post,* November 3, 1966.

[15]*New York Times,* November 23, 1966.

[16]*Ibid.*

[17]Syndicated column appearing in Portland, Maine, *Press Herald,* October 28, 1966.

CHAPTER 7

[1]"The Economic Report of the President," 1964, p. 58.

[2]See Mollie Orshansky, "Counting the Poor: Another Look at the Poverty Profile," *Social Security Bulletin* Vol. 28 (January, 1965) pp. 3–13. "Who's Who Among the Poor: A Demographic View of Poverty," *ibid.* (July, 1965), p. 3–33; and "Recounting the Poor: A Five Year Review," *ibid.,* Vol. 29 (April, 1966), pp. 26–37.

[3]I am indebted to Judge Frank M. Coffin for this insight.

[4]Michael Harrington, *The Other America,* p. 182.

[5]*Ibid.,* p. 183.

[6]1966 *Manpower Report of the President,* p. 25.

[7]Quoted by John Kifner in the *New York Times,* March 16, 1967. The story, which makes a mockery of national full-employment policy, was placed in the nation's leading newspaper on page 55 next to the theater ads.

[8]Statement by Whitney Young in *Senate Hearings Before the Subcommittee on the Executive Reorganization of the Committee on Government Operations: Federal Role in Urban Affairs,* December 14, 1966.

[9]*Congressional Quarterly Weekly Report,* December 23, 1966, p. 3063.

CHAPTER 8

[1]See Evans and Novak, *Lyndon B. Johnson,* p. 8. The time was the battle over the Court-packing plan—early in 1937. Senator Tom Connally of Texas and Vice-President Garner were opposed. Sam Rayburn refused to support it, as, of course, did many liberals. Johnson, an unknown candidate in a special Texas election, unexpectedly embraced the Court plan without reservations (or request from the White House) at a time when most of the President's friends were racing for the lifeboats. . . . Roosevelt was more than gratified. He interrupted a vacation cruise on the Gulf of Mexico to meet Johnson in Galveston the day after the special election.

[2]Daniel P. Moynihan, "The Professionalization of Reform," *Public Interest* (Fall, 1965), Vol. 1, p. 8. Moynihan cites an earlier article by Nathan Glazer in a British journal, *The New Society,* which makes much the same point.

[3]Nathan Glazer, "Why Are the Poor Still With Us?" *Public Interest* (Fall, 1965), Vol. I, p. 80.

[4]Schattschneider, p. 2.

[5]Daniel P. Moynihan, "The Professionalism of Reform."

[6]*Ibid.*

[7]Nathan Glazer, "Why Are the Poor Still With Us?", p. 77.

[8]Joseph P. Lyford, pp. 344–48.

[9]*New York Times Magazine,* November 7, 1965.

[10]Robert B. Semple, Jr., *New York Times,* November 28, 1965.

[11]*New York Times,* December 8, 1966.

[12]We now have the benefit of Richard F. Fenno, Jr.'s definitive study of appropriations politics in Congress, *The Power of the Purse* (Boston, 1966).

[13]Evans and Novak, *Lyndon B. Johnson,* p. 433.

[14]Douglas Cater, "For the Record," *The Reporter,* December 15, 1966.

[15]Daniel P. Moynihan, *"What Is Community Action?",* *Public Interest* (Fall, 1966).

[16]*Ibid.,* p. 6.

[17]*Ibid.,* p. 7. (Italics added.)

[18]*Ibid.,* p. 8.

[19]Evans and Novak, *Lyndon B. Johnson,* p. 430.

[20]Lee Rainwater and William L. Yancey, "Black Families and the White House," *Transaction,* Summer, 1966, p. 6. Rainwater and Yancey subsequently published in book form an expanded version of the *Transaction* article: *The Moynihan Report*

and the Politics of Controversy (M.I.T. Press, 1967). The Rainwater and Yancey case study deserves careful study by social scientists. It not only penetrates deeply into the policy-making process but raises basic questions about the relationships between social science research and the political use of that research.

[21]*Ibid.* Rainwater and Yancey present the details in what seems to be a thoroughly researched case study.

[22]All of the quotations in the three paragraphs above are taken from Daniel P. Moynihan, "The President and the Negro: The Moment Lost," *Commentary*, February, 1967.

[23]Statement by Whitney Young before Senate Subcommittee on Executive Reorganization, December 14, 1966.

[24]See the testimony of Mitchell Sviridoff, originally of New Haven and more recently administrator of human resources in New York City, before the so-called Ribicoff committee on August 22, 1966. Sviridoff, one of the most knowledgeable professional poverty warriors in the nation, told the committee: "I do not think the Office of Economic Opportunity has been able to fulfill one of its original objectives, to act as an effective coordinator for Federal programs at the Federal and local level." *Ibid.*, p. 605.

[25]The study was directed by Dr. Max Wolff at the Center for Urban Education under the sponsorship of Yeshiva University, and was supported by OEO funds. The study found that the educational advantages of the Head Start program tend to disappear as the child moves through the later grades. The study also found that Head Start children fare worse than others when the teacher is ineffective. See report by Robert B. Semple, Jr., *New York Times*, October 22, 1966.

[26]See Secretary Wirtz' keynote address at the first National Conference of the Neighborhood Youth Corps, May, 1966, in St. Louis, Missouri. The Secretary's address has since been published in the Conference Report, pp. 4–8.

[27]*New Republic*, March 25, 1967.

[28]In Krosney, p. 35.

[29]See report by John Kifner, *New York Times*, March 16, 1967.

[30]*New York Times*, March 15, 1967.

CHAPTER 9

[1]For a more extended discussion of incrementalism see Charles E. Lindbolm, *The Policy Making Process* (Englewood Cliffs, N.J., 1968); Aaron Wildavsky, *The Politics of the Budgetary Process* (Boston, 1964); and John C. Donovan, *The Policy Makers* (New York, 1970).

[2]*Ibid.*

[3]U. S., House of Representatives. *Hearings Before the Subcommittees of the Committee on Appropriations: Supplemental Appropriation Bill of 1967*. 89th Cong., 2d Sess., October, 1966, Part 1, p. 39.

[4]The special role of the House Appropriations Subcommittee and the unusual power exercised by a skilled chairman are carefully explored in Richard Fenno's *The Power of the Purse* (Boston, 1966).

[5]*House Appropriations Subcommittee Hearings*, pp. 73–78 and 86–87.

[6]*Ibid.*, pp. 265–267. All of the excerpts from the Mahon-Shriver exchange are taken from these hearings.

[7]*Congressional Quarterly Weekly Reports,* May 20, 1972, p. 1128.

[8]For a more complete analysis of the forces at work within the institutionalized presidency and the congressional coalition during the 1960s see Donovan, *Policy Makers.*

[9]*Congressional Quarterly Almanac,* 1967, p. 1058.

[10]These quotations from the Senate committee report may be found in the *Congressional Quarterly Almanac,* 1967, p. 1067.

[11]For more detail see the *Congressional Quarterly Almanac,* 1968.

[12]The factual details in the preceding paragraphs dealing with 1969 are drawn from the *Congressional Quarterly Almanac,* 1969.

[13]There is a brief review and evaluation of the Legal Services program in Sar A. Levitan, *The Great Society's Poor Law* (Baltimore, 1969). Levitan's study, financed by a grant from the Ford Foundation, does not carry beyond fiscal 1968. Pleading "lack of data," Levitan's evaluation of OEO programs is often ambiguous, to say the least, and it obviously does not include the Nixon years.

[14]See especially articles by Jack Rosenthal, *New York Times,* November 20 and December 15, 1970.

[15]This section is based on the detailed analysis in *Congressional Quarterly Almanac,* 1970.

[16]The exchange between Carlucci and members of the House committee was reported by Jack Rosenthal in the *New York Times,* March 23, 1971.

[17]The details of the legislative situation are drawn from *Congressional Quarterly Weekly Reports,* December 12, 1971, and January 29, 1972.

[18]The material in this section including the quotations from the hearings draws upon an excellent report by Paul Delaney which appeared in the *New York Times,* January 26, 1972.

[19]*Congressional Quarterly Weekly Reports,* February 12, 1972.

[20]*Congressional Quarterly Weekly Reports,* February 26, 1972.

[21]*Congressional Quarterly Weekly Reports,* May 20, 1972.

[22]*Congressional Quarterly Weekly Reports,* May 27, 1972.

[23]*Congressional Quarterly Weekly Reports,* September 9, 1972, and *New York Times,* September 20, 1972.

CHAPTER 10

[1]James L. Sundquist, *Politics and Policy* (Washington, D.C., 1968).

[2]Sar A. Levitan, *The Great Society's Poor Law* (Baltimore, 1969).

[3]Daniel P. Moynihan, *Maximum Feasible Misunderstanding* (New York, 1969).

[4]Kenneth B. Clark and Jeanette Hopkins, *A Relevant War Against Poverty* (New York, 1969).

[5]Levitan, *Great Society's Poor Law*, p. 309.

[6]*Ibid.*, p. x.

[7]*Ibid.*, p. 317.

[8]*Ibid.*, p. ix.

[9]Moynihan, *Maximum Feasible Misunderstanding*, p. 170.

[10]*Ibid.*, p. 203.

[11]*Ibid.*, pp. 196–197.

[12]*Ibid.*, p. 197.

[13]John C. Donovan, "The Technician and Public Policy-Making: Two Inside Views," *Polity* 2, no. 3 (Spring, 1970): 374–379. The essay has since been reprinted in Douglas M. Fox, *The New Urban Politics* (Pacific Palisades, Calif., 1972). The quotation is taken from p. 131 in Fox.

[14]Quoted in Moynihan, *Maximum Feasible Misunderstanding*, p. 97. The original quotation appeared in Richard Blumenthal, "Community Action: The Origins of a Government Program," senior thesis, Harvard College, 1967.

[15]*Ibid.*, p. 96. Italics not in the original.

[16]*Ibid.*, p. 98.

[17]See *New York Times*, October 29, 1967.

[18]Richard Blumenthal, "The Bureaucracy: Anti-Poverty and the Community Action Program," in *American Political Institutions and Public Policy*, ed. Allan P. Sindler (Boston, 1969), p. 167.

[19]Moynihan, *Maximum Feasible Misunderstanding*, p. 87.

[20]Blumenthal, "The Bureaucracy," p. 167.

[21]Note Yarmolinsky's comment:

". . . there is an irony in the failure of the original task force—this author included—to anticipate the violent reaction of poor people and poor neighborhoods to the opportunity to affect their lives through community action programs. In a community as sensitive to the problems of the distribution and transmission of power as Washington, the power potential—constructive and destructive—of the poor themselves was largely overlooked." Adam Yarmolinsky, "The Beginnings of OEO," in *On Fighting Poverty*, ed. James L. Sundquist (New York, 1969), p. 50.

[22]Clark and Hopkins, *Relevant War*, p. 159.

[23]*Ibid.*, Preface, p. vi.

[24]*Ibid.*, p, 248.

[25]*Ibid.*, p. 235.

[26]This was the conclusion of the Clark subcommittee, U.S. Senate in 1967. See Howard Hallman, *Examination of the War on Poverty, Staff and Consultants' Reports for the Subcommittee on Employment, Manpower and Poverty of the Committee on Labor and Public Welfare* IV (Washington, D.C., September, 1967). The report said at one point: "Contrary to the hopes of a few and the fears of many, CAP is not a social revolution" (p. 900).

[27]John H. Strange, "Citizen Participation: Experiences in Community Action and Model Cities Programs," mimeographed first draft, 1972. Strange's article, one of a

series sponsored by the Center for Governmental Studies and the National Science Foundation, is to appear in the *Public Administration Review.*

[27]Ralph M. Kramer, *Participation of the Poor* (Englewood Cliffs, N.J., 1969), p. 267. See also Peter Bachrach and Morton S. Baratz, *Power and Poverty* (New York, 1970).

[28]*Ibid.,* pp. 267–268.

[29]See U.S., Department of Labor, "Highlights of the 1972 Manpower Report," in *Manpower* 4, no. 6 (June, 1972): 10.

[30]*Congressional Quarterly Weekly Reports,* April 8, 1972, pp. 781–785, presents a superb report of who the unemployed were in the early 1970s. It also shows how the technicians compile unemployment statistics, an esoteric exercise little understood outside the guild. Tables 4, 5, and 6 are taken from this report.

[31]The standard used by the Census Bureau in 1969 in estimating the number below the poverty line was an income of $3,475 for a non-farm family of four headed by a husband and $3,197 for a comparable farm family.

[32]See reports by Jack Rosenthal, *New York Times,* November 13, 1971, and July 18, 1972.

[33]Associated Press, dateline Washington, D.C., Portland (Maine) *Press Herald,* July 31, 1972.

[34]The 1960s teach the fundamental lesson that the full employment objective also requires a large-scale comprehensive manpower program. Howard Hallman has argued persuasively that supplementary employment opportunities should be provided through the expenditure of public funds. He has proposed that each increase of ½ percent in the unemployment rate would trigger funds for 200,000 public service jobs, with an estimated cost of 1.5 billion dollars, roughly the cost of one month of the war in Vietnam at its peak. See his *Achieving Full Employment: The Role of Manpower Programs,* Center for Governmental Studies, Pamphlet no. 9 (Washington, D.C., January, 1972).

[35]A letter from Xavier Mena, Deputy Director of the Job Corps, to the author, dated July 27, 1972, reported a total of 4,100,000 enrollees in the Neighborhood Youth Corps for fiscal years 1965 through 1972; total expenditures in the same period exceeded $2.4 billion. The Job Corps during the same period had a cumulative enrollment of 390,000 youth and reported expenditures of $1.775 billion. See also Robert A. Levine, former high-ranking OEO official who described the NYC out-of-school and summer programs as being "cover operations for putting some money into the jeans of poor kids." *The Poor Ye Need Not Have With You* (Cambridge, Mass., 1970).

[36]See U.S., Department of Labor press release 72–352, June 7, 1972.

[37]Alan A. Altshuler, *Community Control* (New York, 1970), p. 184.

[38]Howard Hallman, "Citizen Participation in Urban Community Development," in *Urban Community Development Strategies,* Center for Governmental Studies essays and conference report (Washington, D.C., February, 1972), p. 46.

[39]See Frances Fox Piven and Richard A. Cloward, "How the Federal Government Caused the Welfare Crisis," *Social Policy* (May–June, 1971). The article has since been republished in Fox, *Urban Politics.* Those interested in a more extended development of the Piven-Cloward thesis may wish to read their book, *Regulating the Poor: The Functions of Public Welfare* (New York, 1971).

[41]Fox, *Urban Politics,* p. 228.

[42]See especially Daniel P. Moynihan, "Policy vs. Program in the 70s," *The Public Interest*, no. 20 (Summer, 1970): 90–100.

[43]Lyndon B. Johnson, *The Vantage Point* (New York, 1971).

[44]For a more complete discussion of the problem see John C. Donovan, *The Policy Makers* (New York, 1970).

[45]Peter Marris and Martin Rein, *Dilemmas of Social Reform* (New York, 1967) pp. 231–32.

[46]*Ibid.*, p. 232.

[47]Cf. Sundquist:

"The trouble is that there has been no decision to allocate enough of the nation's resources for employment programs, better education, better housing, better health, better cities, and all the other things that must be done. If the nation fails, this time, to avert calamity, it will not basically be for lack of knowledge. It will be for failure of the nation's political leadership to muster the nation's will."

On Fighting Poverty, p. 250.

[48]Robert A. Levine, who served as Assistant Director for Research, Plans, Programs and Evaluation, OEO, in the latter Johnson years, offers in *The Poor Ye Need Not Have* a spirited and somewhat gossipy defense of the program as seen from the higher echelons of OEO. His biases, which are openly indicated, make his evaluation subjective. Since few of the major critics have approached the program objectively, this does not seem to me a grave defect. There is something to be said for an "evaluator" who makes his biases as explicit as Levine does.

[49]See C. Vann Woodward, "The Ghost of Populism Walks Again," *New York Times Magazine*, June 4, 1972.

[50]Henry J. Schmandt, "Municipal Decentralization," mimeographed first draft, an essay prepared for the Center for Governmental Studies and the National Science Foundation for subsequent publication in *Public Administration Review* (1972).

[51]Charles V. Hamilton, "Impact of Racial, Ethnic and Social Class Politics," mimeographed first draft, an essay prepared for the Center for Governmental Studies and the National Science Foundation for subsequent publication in the *Public Administration Review* (1972).

[52]Kramer, *Participation of the Poor*, p. 273.

[53]Kenneth M. Dolbeare and Murray J. Edelman, *American Politics: Policies, Power and Change* (Lexington, Mass., 1971), offers a searching critique of American politics in the 1960s by examining the public policies which the "system" produced.

SELECT BIBLIOGRAPHY

PUBLIC DOCUMENTS

Advisory Commission on Intergovernmental Relations. *Intergovernmental Relations in the Poverty Program.* Washington, D.C.: U.S. Government Printing Office, 1966.

Manpower Report of the President and *Report on Manpower Requirements,* Resources, Utilization, and Training. Washington, D.C.: U.S. Government Printing Office, 1965, 1972.

Orshansky, Mollie. "Counting the Poor: Another Look at the Poverty Profile." *Social Security Bulletin* 28 (January, 1965): 3–13.

_____. "Who's Who Among the Poor: A Demographic View of Poverty." *Social Security Bulletin* 28 (July, 1965): 3–33.

_____. "Recounting the Poor: A Five Year Review." *Social Security Bulletin* 29 (April, 1966): 26–37.

The President's Task Force on Manpower Conservation. *One-Third of a Nation.* Washington, D.C.: U.S. Government Printing Office, 1964.

U.S. *Congressional Record* CXI.

U.S. House of Representatives. Committee on Appropriations. *Hearings: Supplemental Appropriation Bill, 1967.* 89th Cong., 2d sess., October, 1966, Part I.

_____. Committee on Education and Labor. *Economic Opportunity Act of 1964: Report Number 1458.* 88th Cong., 2d sess., 1964.

_____. Committee on Education and Labor. *Economic Opportunity Amendments of 1965: Opt. Number 428.* 89th Cong., 1st sess., 1965.

_____. Committee on Education and Labor. *Poverty in the United States.* 88th Cong., 2d sess., 1964.

_____. *Hearings Before the Subcommittee on Executive Reorganization of the Committee on Education and Labor: 1966 Amendments to the Economic Opportunity Act of 1964.* 89th Cong., 2d sess., 1966.

_____. *Hearings Before the Subcommittee on the War on Poverty Program of the Committee on Education and Labor: The Economic Opportunity Act of 1964.* 88th Cong., 2d sess., 1964.

U.S. President. (Johnson) "The Economic Report of the President," January 20, 1964. *Public Papers of the Presidents.*

U.S. Senate. Committee on Labor and Public Welfare. *Economic Opportunity Act of 1964: Report Number 1218.* 88th Cong., 2d sess., 1964.

_____. Committee on Labor and Public Welfare. *Examination of the War on Poverty: Staff and Consultants' Reports of the Subcommittee on Employment, Manpower and Poverty* IV. Washington, D.C.: U.S. Government Printing Office, 1967.

_____. *Hearings Before the Subcommittee on Executive Reorganization of the Committee on Government Operations: Federal Role in Urban Affairs.* 89th Cong., 2d sess., 1966.

BOOKS

Altschuler, Alan A. *Community Control.* New York: Pegasus, 1970.

Bachrach, Peter and Morton S. Baratz. *Power and Poverty.* New York: Oxford, 1970.

Bagdikian, Ben H. *In the Midst of Plenty: The Poor in America.* Boston: Beacon Press, 1964.

Bibby, John Franklin and Roger H. Davidson. *On Capitol Hill.* New York: Holt, Rinehart and Winston, 1967.

Bremner, Robert H. *From the Depths: The Discovery of Poverty in the United States.* New York: New York University Press, 1956.

Caudill, Harry M. *Night Comes to the Cumberlands: A Biography of a Depressed Area.* Boston: Little, Brown. 1963.

Clark, Kenneth B. *Dark Ghetto: Dilemmas of Social Power.* New York: Harper and Row, 1965.

_____ and Jeannette Hopkins. *A Relevant War Against Poverty.* New York: Harper and Row, 1969.

Congressional Quarterly Almanac XX-XXVII. Washington, D.C.: Congressional Quarterly, Inc., 1964–1971.

Dahl, Robert Alan. *Who Governs? Democracy and Power in an American City.* New Haven: Yale University Press, 1961.

Dolbeare, Kenneth M. and Murray J. Edelman. *American Politics: Policies, Power, and Change.* Lexington, Mass.: D.C. Heath, 1971.

Donovan, John C. *The Policy Makers.* New York: Pegasus, 1970.

Evans, Rowland, and Robert Novak. *Lyndon B. Johnson: The Exercise of Power.* New York: New American Library, 1966.

Fenno, Richard F., Jr. *The Power of the Purse: Appropriations Politics in Congress.* Boston: Little, Brown, 1966.

Ferman, Louis A., Joyce L. Kornbluh, and Alan Haber, eds. *Poverty in America: A Book of Readings.* Ann Arbor: University of Michigan Press, 1965.

Fishman, Leo, ed. *Poverty and Affluence.* New Haven: Yale University Press, 1966.

Fox, Douglas M., ed. *The New Urban Politics.* Pacific Palisades, Calif.: Goodyear, 1972.

Galbraith, John K. *The Affluent Society.* Boston: Houghton Mifflin, 1958.

Glazer, Nathan, and Daniel P. Moynihan. *Beyond the Melting Pot.* Cambridge, Mass.: M.I.T. Press, 1963.

Gordon, Margaret S. *The Economics of Welfare Politics.* New York: Columbia University Press, 1963.

_____, ed. *Poverty in America.* Berkeley: Chandler, 1965.

Harrington, Michael. *The Other America: Poverty in the United States.* New York: Macmillan, 1962.

Hentoff, Nat. *The New Equality.* New York: Viking Press, 1966.

Johnson, Lyndon B. *The Vantage Point.* New York: Holt, Rinehart and Winston, 1971.

Kramer, Ralph M. *Participation of the Poor*. Englewood Cliffs, N.J.: Prentice-Hall, 1969.

Krosney, Herbert. *Beyond Welfare: Poverty in the Supercity*. New York: Holt, Rinehart and Winston, 1966.

Levine, Robert A. *The Poor Ye Need Not Have With You*. Cambridge, Mass.: M.I.T. Press, 1970.

Levitan, Sar A. *The Great Society's Poor Law*. Baltimore: Johns Hopkins Press, 1969.

Lindblom, Charles E. *The Policy Making Process*. Englewood Cliffs, N.J.: Prentice-Hall, 1968.

Lyford, Joseph P. *The Airtight Cage*. New York: Harper and Row, 1966.

McCormack, Arthur. *World Poverty and the Christian*. New York: Hawthorne Press, 1963.

Marris, Peter, and Martin Rein. *The Dilemmas of Social Reform*. New York: Atherton Press, 1967.

Miller, Herman P. *Rich Man, Poor Man*. New York: Thomas Y. Crowell, 1964.

Moynihan, Daniel P. *Maximum Feasible Misunderstanding*. New York: Free Press, 1969.

Myrdal, Gunnar. *An American Dilemma*. New York: Harper and Row, 1944.

————. *Challenge to Affluence*. New York: Pantheon, 1962.

Neustadt, Richard E. *Presidential Power*. New York: John Wiley and Sons, 1960.

Pearl, Arthur, and Frank Riessman. *New Careers for the Poor: The Nonprofessional in Human Service*. New York: Free Press, 1965.

Piven, Frances F., and Richard A. Cloward. *Regulating the Poor: The Functions of Public Welfare*. New York: Pantheon, 1971.

Rainwater, Lee and William L. Yancey. *The Moynihan Report and the Politics of Controversy*. Cambridge Mass.: M.I.T. Press, 1967.

Ross, Arthur M., and Herbert Hill. *Employment, Race and Poverty*. New York: Harcourt, Brace and World, 1966.

Schattschneider, Elmer E. *The Semisovereign People*. New York: Holt, Rinehart and Winston, 1960.

Schlesinger, Arthur M., Jr. *A Thousand Days*. Boston: Houghton Mifflin, 1965.

Schorr, Alvin L. *Poor Kids*. New York: Basic Books, 1966.

Shostak, Arthur, and William Gomberg, eds. *New Perspectives on Poverty*. Englewood Cliffs, N.J.: Prentice-Hall, 1965.

Silberman, Charles E. *Crisis in Black and White*. New York: Random House, 1964.

Sindler, Allan P., ed. *American Institutions and Public Policy*. Boston: Little, Brown, 1969.

Sundquist, James L. *Politics and Policy*. Washington, D.C.: Brookings, 1968.

————. *On Fighting Poverty*. New York: Basic Books, 1969.

Theobald, Robert. *Free Men and Free Markets*. Garden City, N.Y.: Doubleday, 1965.

————. *Guaranteed Income*. Garden City, N.Y.: Doubleday, 1966.

Wildavsky, Aaron. *The Politics of the Budgetary Process*. Boston: Little, Brown, 1964.

Will, Robert E. and Harold G. Vatter. *Poverty in Affluence: The Social, Political, and Economic Dimensions of Poverty in the United States.* New York: Harcourt, Brace and World, 1965.

ARTICLES AND PERIODICALS

Arnold, Mark R. "Behind a Demonstration: Some Planning, Much Anger." *The National Observer,* May 9, 1966, page 6.

Carter, Barbara. "Sargent Shriver and the Role of the Poor." *The Reporter,* May 5, 1966, pages 17–20.

_____. "The Great Society: A Man with a Problem." *The Reporter,* May 20, 1965, pages 32–33.

Cater, Douglass G. "For the Record." *The Reporter,* December 15, 1966, pages 24–26.

Cloward, Richard A. "The War on Poverty: Are the Poor Left Out?" *The Nation,* August 2, 1965, pages 55–60.

Congressional Quarterly Weekly Report XXIV–XXX, 1966–1972.

Dale, Edwin L., Jr. "Uncle Sam's $50 Billion Surplus." *New York Times Magazine,* November 7, 1965, pages 32–33.

Donovan, John C. "The Technician and Public Policy Making: Two Inside Views." *Polity* 3 (Spring, 1970): 374–397.

Glazer, Nathan. "Why are the Poor Still With Us?" *Public Interest,* no. 1 (Fall, 1965): 6–16.

_____. "The Grand Design of the Poverty Program (To Produce a Creative Disorder)." *New York Times Magazine,* February 27, 1966, pages 21, 64–72.

Haddad, William F. "Mr. Shriver and the Savage Politics of Poverty." *Harper's,* December, 1965, pages 43–50.

Hamilton, Charles V. "Impact of Racial, Ethnic and Social Class Politics." Mimeographed draft to appear in *Public Administration Review* (1972).

Harrington, Michael. "The Politics of Poverty." *Dissent* XII (Autumn, 1965): 412–430.

MacDonald, Dwight. "Our Invisible Poor." Sidney Hillman Foundation, New York. (Reprinted from the *New Yorker,* January 19, 1963.)

Moynihan, Daniel P. "The Professionalization of Reform." *Public Interest,* no. 1 (Fall, 1965): 6–16.

_____. "What is Community Action?" *Public Interest,* no. 5 (Fall, 1966): 3–8.

_____. "The President and the Negro: The Moment Lost." *Commentary* 43 (February, 1967): 31–45.

_____. "Policy Versus Program in the '70s." *Public Interest,* no. 20 (Summer, 1970): 90–100.

"Poverty in America." *The New Leader* XLVII (March 30, 1964): 7–23, in five articles: "Our Permanent Paupers" by Paul Jacobs; "The New Poor" by A. H. Raskin; "Statistics and Reality" by Herman P. Miller; "A Glib Fallacy" by Michael Harrington; and "Poverty and Pecksniff" by Irving Kristol.

Rainwater, Lee, and William L. Yancey. "Black Families and the White House." *Transaction* 3 (Summer, 1966): 6–11, 48–52.

Schmandt, Henry J. "Municipal Decentralization." Mimeographed draft to appear in *Public Administration Review* (1972).

Silberman, Charles E. "The Mixed Up War on Poverty (Technology and the Labor Movement)." *Fortune*, August, 1956, pages 156–161, 218–226.

Strange, John H. "Citizen Participation: Experience in Community Action and Model Cities Programs." Mimeographed draft to appear in *Public Administration Review* (1972).

Witcover, Jules, and Erwain Knoll. "Politics and the Poor: Shriver's Second Thoughts." *The Reporter*, December 30, 1965, pages 23–25.

Woodward, C. Vann. "The Ghost of Populism Walks Again." *New York Times Magazine*, June 4, 1972.

REPORTS

Chamber of Commerce of the United States. Task Force on Economic Growth and Opportunity. *The Concept of Poverty*. Washington, D.C., 1965.

Hallman, Howard. *Achieving Full Employment: The Role of Manpower Programs*. Center for Governmental Studies pamphlet no. 9, January, 1972.

_____. "Citizen Participation in Urban Community Development." In *Urban Community Development Strategies*, essays and conference report. Center for Governmental Studies, Washington, D.C., February, 1972.

Harlem Youth Opportunities Unlimited. *Youth in the Ghetto: A Study of the Consequences of Powerlessness and a Blueprint for Change*. New York, 1964.

Ornati, Oscar. *Poverty in America*. National Policy Committee on Pockets of Poverty, Washington, D.C., 1964.

Southern Regional Council. *Federal "Anti-Poverty" Programs: Present and Pending*. Atlanta, Georgia, 1965.

NEWSPAPERS

Christian Science Monitor.

New York Times.

Press Herald (Portland, Maine).

Wall Street Journal.

Washington Post.

UNPUBLISHED MATERIAL

Blumenthal, Richard. "Community Action: The Origins of a Government Program." Senior thesis, Harvard College, 1967.

Smith, Brian. "The Role of the Poor in the Poverty Program: The Origin and Development of Maximum Feasible Participation." Master's thesis, Columbia University, 1966.

INDEX